Math in F☉CUS®

Singapore Math®
by Marshall Cavendish

Extra Practice and Homework

Program Consultant
Dr. Fong Ho Kheong

Author
Chelvi Ramakrishnan

 **Marshall Cavendish** Education

U.S. Distributor

 **Houghton Mifflin Harcourt.**
The Learning Company™

Grade 5A

© 2020 Marshall Cavendish Education Pte Ltd

Published by Marshall Cavendish Education
Times Centre, 1 New Industrial Road, Singapore 536196
Customer Service Hotline: (65) 6213 9688
US Office Tel: (1-914) 332 8888 | Fax: (1-914) 332 8882
E-mail: cs@mceducation.com
Website: www.mceducation.com

Distributed by
Houghton Mifflin Harcourt
125 High Street
Boston, MA 02110
Tel: 617-351-5000
Website: www.hmhco.com/programs/math-in-focus

First published 2020

ISBN 978-0-358-10306-6

Printed in Singapore

1 2 3 4 5 6 7 8   1401   25 24 23 22 21 20
4500759430   A B C D E

The cover image shows a giant panda.
Giant pandas have thick, fluffy, black and white fur. They live in bamboo forests in China. Bamboo accounts for over 95% of their diet. Unlike other bears, pandas do not hibernate in the winter. They migrate to areas with warmer temperatures depending on the season. They used to be endangered in the past, but are now protected and their numbers are increasing once again.

Contents

© 2020 Marshall Cavendish Education Pte Ltd

Preface

Welcome!

Math in Focus® Extra Practice and Homework is written to be used with the
Math in Focus® Student Edition, to support your learning.

This book provides activities and problems that closely follow what you have learned in the Student Edition.

- In **Activities**, you practice the concepts and skills you learned in the Student Edition, so that you can master the concepts and build your confidence.

- In **MATH JOURNAL**, you reflect on your thinking when you write down your thoughts about the math concepts you learned.

- In **PUT ON YOUR THINKING CAP!**, you develop your problem-solving and critical thinking skills, and challenge yourself to apply concepts in different ways.

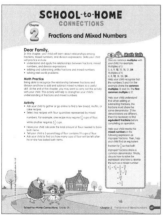

This book also includes **SCHOOL-to-HOME CONNECTIONS**. Each family letter summarizes the learning objectives and the key mathematical vocabulary you are using. The letter also includes one or more activities that your family can do with you to support your learning further.

BLANK

SCHOOL-to-HOME
CONNECTIONS

Chapter 1

Whole Numbers and The Four Operations

Dear Family,

In this chapter, your child will learn about reading and writing large numbers and using operations to solve word problems. Skills your child will practice include:

- reading and writing numbers within 10,000,000
- multiplying by tens, hundreds, thousands, and powers of tens
- dividing by tens, hundreds, or thousands
- multiplying and dividing by 2-digit numbers fluently
- using order of operations to solve expressions
- solving real-world problems

Math Practice

Being able to work with large numbers is a useful skill in everyday life. At the end of this chapter, you may want to carry out these activities with your child. These activities will help your child practice using order of operations and to strengthen his or her number sense.

Activity 1

- Ask your child to roll a number cube several times and write the numbers on a piece of paper.
- Use the numbers to write an expression that includes parentheses and all four operations.
- Have your child use the order of operations to solve the expression.

Activity 2

- Have your child identify familiar cities, countries, or places he or she would like to visit.
- Use library resources or go online to find the population of each location and record the numbers on a piece of paper.
- Ask your child to read each number aloud and order the numbers from least to greatest.

Activity 3

- Have your child identify a topic of interest that involves numbers up to 10 million. For example, your child may be interested in learning about populations of social insects, such as termites or ants. The number of insects in some colonies can be millions or more.
- Use library resources or go online to learn more about the topic.

Math Talk

Have your child draw a place-value chart including millions. Then, write a digit in each place, and ask your child to read the value of each digit. Next, ask your child to write the number in **expanded form**. For example, the number 5,634,213 in expanded form:

$$5,634,213 = 5,000,000 + 600,000 \\ + 30,000 + 4,000 \\ + 200 + 10 + 3$$

Help your child understand that an **expression** is similar to a word phrase, but it uses numbers in place of words and operation symbols, such as +, −, ×, and ÷. For example, $5 + (5 \times 4) \div 2$ is an expression. Invite your child to explain how to solve the expression using the **order of operations**. Explain that in this example, he or she must work within the parentheses first. Then, he or she multiplies and divides from left to right. Finally, he or she adds and subtracts from left to right.

$5 + (5 \times 4) \div 2$
$= 5 + 20 \div 2$
$= 5 + 10$
$= 15$
So, $5 + (5 \times 4) \div 2 = 15$.

BLANK

Name: _____   Date: _____

Chapter
1

Extra Practice and Homework
Whole Numbers and The Four Operations

Activity 1   Numbers to 10,000,000

Complete the table. Then, write the number in standard form and word form.

1

Millions	Hundred Thousands	Ten Thousands	Thousands	Hundreds	Tens	Ones
1,000,000 1,000,000 1,000,000 1,000,000 1,000,000 1,000,000 1,000,000 1,000,000 1,000,000	100,000	10,000 10,000 10,000 10,000 10,000	1,000 1,000 1,000 1,000 1,000 1,000	100 100 100	10 10 10 10	1 1

	Standard Form	Word Form
▢ millions		
▢ hundred thousand		
▢ ten thousands		
▢ thousands		
▢ hundreds		
▢ tens		
▢ ones		

Number in standard form: _____

Number in word form: _____

_____

Write the number in standard form and word form.

② Millions	Hundred Thousands	Ten Thousands	Thousands	Hundreds	Tens	Ones
1,000,000 1,000,000 1,000,000	100,000 100,000	10,000 10,000 10,000 10,000				

Number in standard form: _____

Number in word form: _____

Write each number in standard form.

③ two million, one hundred fifty-six thousand, four _____

④ five million, two hundred thirty-eight thousand _____

⑤ seven million, one hundred fifty thousand _____

⑥ six million, sixty thousand, fifty _____

⑦ three million, three _____

Write each number in word form.

⑧ 5,050,000 _____

⑨ 8,147,600 _____

10 7,230,014 _____

_____

11 5,192,622 _____

_____

12 9,009,009 _____

Fill in each blank. Use the place-value chart to help you.

Hundred Thousands	Ten Thousands	Thousands	Hundreds	Tens	Ones
100,000 100,000 100,000	10,000 10,000 10,000 10,000	1,000 1,000 1,000 1,000 1,000	100 100		1
3	4	5,	2	0	1

In 345,201

13 a the digit 3 stands for _____.

b the value of the digit 3 is _____.

14 a the digit 4 stands for _____.

b the value of the digit 4 is _____.

15 a the digit 5 stands for _____.

b the value of the digit 5 is _____.

Write the value of each digit in the correct blank.

16

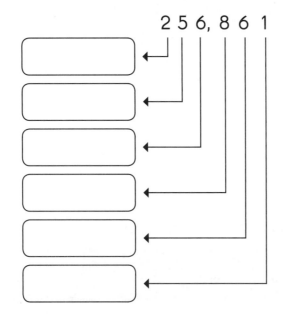

2 5 6, 8 6 1

Fill in each blank.

In 346,812

17 the digit 3 stands for _____.

18 the digit 6 stands for _____.

Write the value of the digit 2 in each number.

19 3**2**9,051 _____

20 903,5**2**1 _____

21 71**2**,635 _____

22 **2**58,169 _____

Fill in each blank.

23 In 320,187, the digit _____ is in the thousands place.

24 In 835,129, the digit 8 is in the _____ place.

25 In 348,792, the digit 4 is in the _____ place.

Complete each expanded form.

26 $153{,}420 = 100{,}000 + \underline{\hspace{3cm}} + 3{,}000 + 400 + 20$

27 $760{,}300 = \underline{\hspace{3cm}} + 60{,}000 + 300$

28 $951{,}058 = 900{,}000 + 50{,}000 + \underline{\hspace{3cm}} + 50 + 8$

29 $700{,}000 + 8{,}000 + 500 + 4 = \underline{\hspace{3cm}}$

30 $200{,}000 + 2{,}000 + 10 = \underline{\hspace{3cm}}$

31 $500{,}000 + 60{,}000 + 3{,}000 + 100 + 40 + 3 = \underline{\hspace{3cm}}$

Fill in each blank. Use the place-value chart to help you.

Millions	Hundred Thousands	Ten Thousands	Thousands	Hundreds	Tens	Ones
1,000,000	100,000 100,000 100,000 100,000 100,000		1,000 1,000 1,000 1,000 1,000 1,000 1,000	100 100 100	10 10 10 10 10	1 1 1 1 1 1 1 1 1
1,	5	0	8,	3	6	9

In 1,508,369

32 a   the digit 1 stands for \underline{\hspace{3cm}}.

   b   the value of the digit 1 is \underline{\hspace{3cm}}.

33 a   the digit 8 stands for \underline{\hspace{3cm}}.

   b   the value of the digit 8 is \underline{\hspace{3cm}}.

34   the digit 0 is in the \underline{\hspace{4cm}} place.

Write the value of each digit in the correct blank.

35

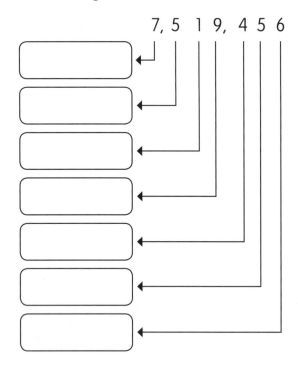

7, 5 1 9, 4 5 6

Fill in each blank.

36 In 5,420,000, the digit 5 is in the _____ place.

37 In 1,077,215, the digit in the hundred thousands place is _____.

38 In 9,400,210, the digit 9 stands for _____.

Complete each expanded form.

39 4,130,000 = _____ + 100,000 + 30,000

40 6,123,750 = 6,000,000 + 100,000 + 20,000 + 3,000 + 700 + _____

41 7,550,100 = 7,000,000 + _____ + 50,000 + 100

42 5,000,000 + 200,000 + 7,000 + 70 = _____

43 3,000,000 + 20,000 + 9,000 + 100 + 5 = _____

© 2020 Marshall Cavendish Education Pte Ltd

Read the clues to find each number.

44 It is a 6-digit number.
The value of the digit 5 is 500,000.
The digit 4 is next to the digit in the hundred thousands place.
The least digit is in the thousands place.
The value of the digit 8 is 800.
The digit 2 is in the ones place.
The digit 7 stands for 70.

The number is _____.

45 It is a 7-digit number.
The value of the digit 7 is 700.
The greatest digit is in the millions place.
The digit 1 is next to the digit in the millions place.
The value of the digit 8 is 80.
The value of the digit 3 is 3.
The digit 5 is in the thousands place.
The digit 6 stands for 60,000.

The number is _____.

46 It is a 7-digit number.
The value of the digit 6 is 60,000.
The least digit is in the hundreds place.
The digit 8 is in between the digits in the ten thousands and hundreds place.
The digit 5 is in the ones and hundred thousands place.
The value of the digit 7 is 70.
The digit 2 stands for 2,000,000.

The number is _____.

47 It is a 6-digit number.
The greatest digit is in the ten thousands place.
The digit 0 is in between the digits in the tens and thousands place.

A possible number is _____.

48 It is a 6-digit number.
The digit 7 is in the hundred thousands place.
The digit 3 is in the hundreds place.

A possible number is _____.

49 It is a 7-digit number.
The value of the digit 1 is 10.
The value of the digit 8 is 80,000.

A possible number is _____.

50 It is a 7-digit number.
The digit 2 stands for 2,000,000.
The digit 6 stands for 6.

A possible number is _____.

51 It is a 7-digit number.
The least digit is in the hundreds place.
The digit 2 is in between the digits in the millions and ten thousands place.

A possible number is _____.

Chapter 1

Extra Practice and Homework
Whole Numbers and The Four Operations

Activity 2   Multiplying by Tens, Hundreds, Thousands, and Powers of Tens

Fill in each blank.

1 **a** $36 \times 10 =$ _____

b $409 \times 10 =$ _____

c $6{,}320 \times 10 =$ _____

d $5{,}200 \times 10 =$ _____

2 **a**   _____ $\times\, 96 = 960$

b $10 \times$ _____ $= 700$

c $514 \times$ _____ $= 5{,}140$

d   _____ $\times\, 10 = 6{,}000$

3 **a** 65×40

b $39 \times 50 =$ _____

$= 65 \times$ _____ $\times\, 10$

$=$ _____ $\times\, 10$

$=$ _____

c $250 \times 60 =$ _____

d $2,854 \times 70 =$ _____

4 a $52 \times 100 =$ _____

b $40 \times 100 =$ _____

c $95 \times 100 =$ _____

d $217 \times 100 =$ _____

e $315 \times 100 =$ _____

f $3,810 \times 100 =$ _____

g $5 \times 1,000 =$ _____

h $70 \times 1,000 =$ _____

i $400 \times 1,000 =$ _____

j $603 \times 1,000 =$ _____

k $8,032 \times 1,000 =$ _____

l $9,097 \times 1,000 =$ _____

5 a _____ $\times 19 = 1,900$

b $3,151 \times$ _____ $= 315,100$

c _____ $\times 1,000 = 568,000$

d $280 \times$ _____ $= 280,000$

e $1,000 \times$ _____ $= 35,000$

f _____ $\times 1,000 = 1,872,000$

6 **a** 9×800

$= 9 \times$ _____ $\times 100$

$=$ _____ $\times 100$

$=$ _____

b $75 \times 200 =$ _____

c $123 \times 600 =$ _____

d $8 \times 5,000 =$ _____

e $17 \times 9,000 =$ _____

f $105 \times 4,000 =$ _____

7 **a** $10 \times 54 =$ _____

b $932 \times 100 =$ _____

c $1,000 \times 4,732 =$ _____

d $1,092 \times 80 =$ _____

e $4,000 \times 90 =$ _____

f $700 \times 18 =$ _____

g $162 \times 500 =$ _____

h $634 \times 2,000 =$ _____

8 $36 \times 10^2 = 36 \times ($ _____ $\times$ _____ $)$

$= 36 \times$ _____

$=$ _____

9 $17 \times 10^2 = 17 \times ($ _____ $\times$ _____ $)$

$= 17 \times$ _____

$=$ _____

10 $98 \times 10^2 = 98 \times ($ _____ $\times$ _____ $)$

$= 98 \times$ _____

$=$ _____

11 $432 \times 10^2 = 432 \times ($ _____ $\times$ _____ $)$

$= 432 \times$ _____

$=$ _____

12 $210 \times 10^2 = 210 \times ($ _____ $\times$ _____ $)$

$= 210 \times$ _____

$=$ _____

13 $607 \times 10^2 = 607 \times ($ _____ $\times$ _____ $)$

$= 607 \times$ _____

$=$ _____

Multiply.

14 $625 \times 10^2 = $ _____

15 $1{,}000 \times 10^2 = $ _____

16 $5{,}118 \times 10^2 = $ _____

Solve.

17 Jacob multiplied $3{,}406 \times 10^2$ in the following way:

$$3{,}406 \times 10^2 = 3{,}406 \times 10 \times 2$$
$$= 34{,}060 \times 2$$
$$= 68{,}120$$

Is Jacob's method correct? If not, explain the error and show the correct way to find the answer.

Fill in each blank.

18 $62 \times 10^3 = 62 \times ($ _____ $\times$ _____ $\times$ _____ $)$

$= 62 \times$ _____

$=$ _____

19 $53 \times 10^3 = 53 \times ($ _____ $\times$ _____ $\times$ _____ $)$

$= 53 \times$ _____

$=$ _____

20 $74 \times 10^3 = 74 \times ($ _____ $\times$ _____ $\times$ _____ $)$

$= 74 \times$ _____

$=$ _____

21 $318 \times 10^3 = 318 \times ($ _____ $\times$ _____ $\times$ _____ $)$

$= 318 \times$ _____

$=$ _____

22 $490 \times 10^3 = 490 \times ($ _____ $\times$ _____ $\times$ _____ $)$

$= 490 \times$ _____

$=$ _____

23 $708 \times 10^3 = 708 \times ($ _____ $\times$ _____ $\times$ _____ $)$

$= 708 \times$ _____

$=$ _____

Multiply.

24 $907 \times 10^3 =$ _____

25 $4{,}125 \times 10^3 =$ _____

26 $2{,}000 \times 10^3 =$ _____

Fill in each blank with "10", "10², or "10³".

27 310×10^2 is the same as $31 \times$ _____.

28 $6{,}000 \times 10 = 600 \times$ _____

29 $405 \times$ _____ $= 4{,}050 \times 10^2$

30 To change from kilograms to grams, multiply by _____.

Extra Practice and Homework Grade 5A

Chapter 1

Extra Practice and Homework
Whole Numbers and The Four Operations

Activity 3 Dividing by Tens, Hundreds, and Thousands

Fill in each blank.

1 a   100 ÷ 10 = _____

b   230 ÷ 10 = _____

c   4,200 ÷ 10 = _____

d   30,750 ÷ 10 = _____

2 a   91,020 ÷ 10 = _____

b   1,050 ÷ _____ = 105

c   30,500 ÷ _____ = 3,050

d   _____ ÷ 10 = 1,965

3 a   8,430 ÷ 30

= 8,430 ÷ _____ ÷ 3

= _____ ÷ 3

= _____

b   3,000 ÷ 60 = _____

c   7,280 ÷ 40 = _____

d   34,230 ÷ 70 = _____

4 **What is the code for the safe? Divide. Then, match each number to an answer to find out.**

3,400 ÷ 100 = _____

8

518,000 ÷ 1,000 = _____

3

6,000 ÷ 100 = _____

0

38,000 ÷ 1,000 = _____

4

7,500 ÷ _____ = 75

7

_____ ÷ 100 = 20

1

_____ ÷ 100 = 930

9

_____ ÷ 1,000 = 4,150

2

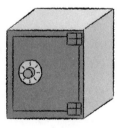

___	___	___	___	___	___	___	___
34	38	518	60	2,000	93,000	4,150,000	100

5 **a** 680 ÷ 10 = _____

b 200,000 ÷ 100 = _____

c 900 ÷ 100 = _____

d 8,000 ÷ 1,000 = _____

e 1,190 ÷ 70 = _____

f 5,000 ÷ 200 = _____

g 51,000 ÷ 300 = _____

h 435,600 ÷ 200 = _____

i 92,000 ÷ 4,000 = _____

j 534,000 ÷ 2,000 = _____

6 **a** $600 \div 300$

　　　$= 600 \div$ _____ $\div 3$

　　　$=$ _____ $\div 3$

　　　$=$ _____

b $24,000 \div 40 =$ _____

c $83,700 \div 900 =$ _____

d $150,000 \div 500 =$ _____

e $9,000 \div 3,000 =$ _____

f $40,000 \div 8,000 =$ _____

g $133,000 \div 7,000 =$ _____

h $40,000 \div$ _____ $= 800$

Solve.

7 What is wrong with the equation?

$$\boxed{2,500} \div \boxed{20} = 1,250$$

_____

Change one of the numbers in the blanks to get the given

answer. _____

Chapter 1

Extra Practice and Homework
Whole Numbers and The Four Operations

Activity 4 Multiplying and Dividing by 2-Digit Numbers Fluently

Multiply. Show your work. Estimate to check that each answer is reasonable.

1 $23 \times 17 =$ _____

2 $35 \times 31 =$ 1086

```
  1
  35
× 31
────
  36
1,050
1,086
```

3 $43 \times 22 =$ _____

4 $59 \times 42 =$ 2,478

```
  1
  59
× 42
────
 118
2,360
2,478
```

5 $91 \times 14 =$ _____

6 $96 \times 15 =$ 1,440

```
 3
 96
× 15
────
 480
 960
1,440
```

7 $456 \times 57 =$ _____

8 $510 \times 35 =$ _17,850_

$$
\begin{array}{r}
510 \\
\times\ 35 \\
\hline
2550 \\
15,300 \\
\hline
17,850
\end{array}
$$

9 $556 \times 47 =$ _____

10 $614 \times 31 =$ _18,420_

$$
\begin{array}{r}
614 \\
\times\ 31 \\
\hline
614 \\
18,420
\end{array}
$$

11 $750 \times 63 =$ _____

12 $843 \times 25 =$ _16,860_

$$
\begin{array}{r}
843 \\
\times\ 25 \\
\hline
4,215 \\
16,860
\end{array}
$$

13 $1,970 \times 23 =$ _____

14 $2,550 \times 58 =$ _____

15 $3,610 \times 64 =$ _____

16 $4,563 \times 29 =$ _____

17 $5,193 \times 35 =$ _____

18 $8,142 \times 16 =$ _____

Divide. Show your work. Estimate to check that each answer is reasonable.

19 $34 \div 20 =$ _____

20 $65 \div 40 =$ _____

21 $80 \div 60 =$ _____

22 $190 \div 90 =$ _____

23 $360 \div 50 =$ _____

24 $590 \div 30 =$ _____

25 $3,300 \div 90 = $ _____

26 $7,500 \div 80 = $ _____

27 $48 \div 12 = $ _____

28 $98 \div 14 = $ _____

29 $364 \div 14 = $ _____

30 $850 \div 17 = $ _____

31 9,600 ÷ 15 = _____

32 5,004 ÷ 18 = _____

33 51 ÷ 15 = _____

34 85 ÷ 12 = _____

35 546 ÷ 25 = _____

36 720 ÷ 28 = _____

Extra Practice and Homework Grade 5A

37 $3{,}216 \div 22 =$ _____

38 $4{,}250 \div 16 =$ _____

Divide. Use an area model to help you.

39 $936 \div 43$

40 $6{,}028 \div 24$

41 $8,012 \div 36 =$

Solve.

42 What is the least possible 3-digit number that gives a remainder of 3 when divided by 15?

43 What is the least possible number that can be added to 653 to make the result divisible by 9?

Chapter 1
Extra Practice and Homework
Whole Numbers and The Four Operations

Activity 5   Order of Operations

Find the value of each of the following without using a calculator.
Then, use your scientific calculator to check each answer.

1 28 + 19 − 6

2 100 − 26 + 15

3 6 × 5 ÷ 2

4 960 ÷ 30 × 2

5 64 + 16 ÷ 8

6 42 + 30 × 7

7 280 − 75 ÷ 5

8 (35 − 11) × 2

9 $(42 + 60) \div 6$

10 $30 \times (80 - 65)$

11 $132 \div (4 + 2)$

12 $12 + 16 - 8 + 3$

13 $40 - 12 + 17 - 6$

14 $80 \times 40 \div 10 \div 2$

15 $360 \div 10 \times 6 \div 3$

16 $63 - 4 \times 10 \div 5$

17 $85 - 6 \times 2 + 4$

18 $28 \div 4 + 3 \times 6$

19 $15 \times 72 \div (9 \div 3)$

20 $59 - 40 \div (5 \times 8)$

21 $17 + (24 + 16) \div 5$

22 $(37 + 53) - 12 \times 5$

23 $297 - 108 \div 9 \times 3 + 8$

24 $548 \div 2 + 3 \times 16 - 60$

25 $(85 + 95) \div 5 \times (10 - 7)$

26 $(44 + 33) \times (25 - 15) \div 5$

27 $500 - (140 + 36) \times 6 \div (4 - 1)$

28 $600 - 270 \div (6 + 24) \times (11 - 9)$

29 $8 \times (76 - 12 \times 4) \div (8 \div 2)$

30 $(40 + 215 - 77) \times (9 \div 3) - 20$

Name: _____ Date: _____

Chapter 1

Extra Practice and Homework
Whole Numbers and The Four Operations

Activity 6 Real-World Problems: Four Operations of Whole Numbers

Solve. Show your work.

1. There were 918 yellow chairs and blue chairs in all in a hall. The blue chairs were arranged in 36 rows with 12 chairs in each row. The yellow chairs were arranged in rows of 18. How many rows of yellow chairs were there?

You can use the four-step problem-solving model to help you.

Solve. Show your work. Draw bar models to help you.

2 Brooke and Samuel had the same number of marbles. Brooke gave away 20 marbles and Samuel gave away 44 marbles. Brooke then had 3 times as many marbles as Samuel. How many marbles did Brooke and Samuel each have at first?

3 Julia and Evan each had the same length of ribbon. They used their ribbons to make identical bows. Julia made 12 bows and had 128 centimeters of ribbon left. Evan made 9 bows and had 176 centimeters of ribbon left. How many bows could Evan make with the ribbon he had left?

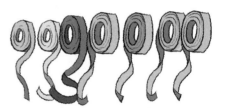

4 Ms. Hall bought 120 greetings cards at 40 for $24.99. Mr. Nelson bought the same number of greetings cards at 30 for $20.95. What was the difference between the amounts that Ms. Hall and Mr. Nelson paid?

5 Ms. Kim had 2,356 beads and Mr. White had 1,176 beads at first. After they each used an equal number of beads, Ms. Kim had 3 times as many beads left as Mr. White. How many beads did each of them use?

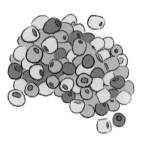

6 Ms. Myers paid $3,600 altogether for the equipment, furniture, and decorations in her restaurant. The equipment cost $500 more than the furniture. The cost of the furniture was twice as much as the cost of the decorations. How much did the equipment cost?

7 There were 4,342 buttons in all in Bags A, B, and C. There were 18 more buttons in Bag B than in Bag A. There were 3 times as many buttons in Bag C as in Bag B. How many buttons were there in Bag A?

8 Luke had 135 sticky labels, Vicente had 990 sticky labels, and Haley had 570 sticky labels. After Haley gave an equal number of sticky labels to both boys, Vicente had 4 times as many sticky labels as Luke. How many sticky labels did Haley have left?

1 **Mathematical Habit 6 Use precise mathematical language**

Ms. Jones, the General Manager of Company A, and Mr. Miller, the General Manager of Company B, each wrote a cheque for $1,280,975.

MC Bank   Date 15 Jan 2020

Payee ___Alex Lee___

The sum of ___One million, two hundred___

thousands eighty thousands, nine hundred $ | 1, 280, 975 |

seventy-five dollars only

                                        Signature: _Lily Jones_

Cheque No.   Bank Branch No.   Account No.

1:7"573842"•2375…°°°,:30005618891.¨•

MC Bank   Date 15 Jan 2020

Payee ___Maria Robinson___

The sum of ___One million, two hundred___

eighty thousand, nine hundred $ | 1, 280, 975 |

seventy-five dollars only

                                        Signature: _Aaron Miller_

Cheque No.   Bank Branch No.   Account No.

1:7"573824"•2375…°°°,:30005618819.¨•

---

a Who wrote the amount in words wrongly?

_____

b Explain the mistake.

_____

_____

MATH JOURNAL

2 | **Mathematical Habit 2** Use mathematical reasoning

Find the value of each of the following equations without using a calculator.

Equation 1 $\quad 35 \div 5 + 67 \times 20 - 13$

Equation 2 $\quad (24 \div 8) + 5 \times (70 - 11 \times 4) \div 2$

Owen's solutions:

Equation 1
$$\begin{aligned}
&35 \div 5 + 67 \times 20 - 13 \\
&= 7 + 1{,}340 - 13 \\
&= 1{,}347 - 13 \\
&= 1{,}334
\end{aligned}$$

Equation 2
$$\begin{aligned}
&(24 \div 8) + 5 \times (70 - 11 \times 4) \div 2 \\
&= 3 + 350 - 44 \div 2 \\
&= 3 + 350 - 22 \\
&= 353 - 22 \\
&= 331
\end{aligned}$$

a Which of Owen's solutions is incorrect? Why?

b Show the correct work.

1 **Mathematical Habit** **7** **Make use of structure**

Study the following.

$4 \blacklozenge 3 = 4 + 44 + 444$
$ = 492$

$4 \blacklozenge 4 = 4 + 44 + 444 + 4{,}444$
$ = 4{,}936$

$4 \blacklozenge 5 = 4 + 44 + 444 + 4{,}444 + 44{,}444$
$ = 49{,}380$

$4 \blacklozenge 6 = 4 + 44 + 444 + 4{,}444 + 44{,}444 + 444{,}444$
$ = 493{,}824$

Find the last four digits of $4 \blacklozenge 10$. Show your work.

2 **Mathematical Habit** **6** **Use precise mathematical language**

Use +, −, ×, and ÷ to write an equation which gives an answer of 7. Put in parentheses if necessary.

$$4 \bigcirc 4 \bigcirc 4 \bigcirc 4 \bigcirc 4 = 7$$

3 **Mathematical Habit** **7** **Make use of structure**

Carla sat in a hall. There were 5 rows of seats behind her and 13 rows of seats in front of her. There were 21 seats to her left and 3 seats to her right in her row. Each row had an equal number of seats. How many seats were there in the hall?

SCHOOL-to-HOME
CONNECTIONS

Chapter 2
Fractions and Mixed Numbers

Dear Family,

In this chapter, your child will learn about relationships among fractions, mixed numbers, and division expressions. Skills your child will practice include:

- understand and apply the relationships between fractions, mixed numbers, and division expressions
- adding and subtracting unlike fractions and mixed numbers
- solving real-world problems

Math Practice

Being able to recognize the relationship between fractions and division and how to add and subtract mixed numbers is a useful skill. At the end of this chapter, you may want to carry out this activity with your child. This activity will help to strengthen your child's understanding of fractions and mixed numbers.

Activity

- Ask your child to gather or go online to find a few bread, muffin, or cake recipes.
- Select two recipes with flour quantities represented by mixed numbers. For example, one recipe may require $1\frac{1}{4}$ cups of flour, while another requires $2\frac{1}{2}$ cups.
- Have your child calculate the total amount of flour needed to bake both items.
- Tell your child a 5-pound bag of flour contains 19 cups of flour.
- Ask your child to find out how many cups of flour will be left after he or she has baked both items.

Math Talk

Discuss common **multiples** with your child. For example:
Multiples of 3:
3, 6, 9, **12**, 15, 18, 21, **24** …
Multiples of 4:
4, 8, **12**, 16, 20, **24** …
Help your child recognize that the numbers 3 and 4 in the example share the **common multiples** 12 and 24. The **first common multiple** is 12.

Help your child understand that when adding or subtracting fractions, the fractions must share the same denominator. If the denominators are different, then it is necessary to find **equivalent fractions** before completing an operation.

Help your child rewrite the **mixed numbers** in the following expression as improper fractions. Then, help your child find an equivalent fraction for $\frac{5}{2}$ so that both improper fractions share a common denominator. Finally, discuss how to solve the expression and how to rewrite the sum as a mixed number.

$$2\frac{1}{2} + 3\frac{1}{4} = \frac{5}{2} + \frac{13}{4}$$
$$= \frac{10}{4} + \frac{13}{4}$$
$$= \frac{23}{4}$$
$$= 5\frac{3}{4}$$

BLANK

Chapter 2

Extra Practice and Homework
Fractions and Mixed Numbers

Activity 1 Fractions, Mixed Numbers, and Division Expressions

Fill in each blank.

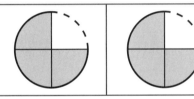 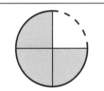

_____ ÷ _____ = ▢/▢

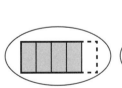 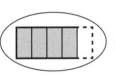 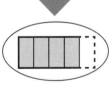 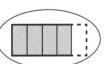 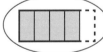

_____ ÷ _____ = ▢/▢

Rewrite each division expression as a fraction.

3 $5 \div 7 = \dfrac{\boxed{}}{\boxed{}}$

4 $3 \div 10 = \dfrac{\boxed{}}{\boxed{}}$

5 $4 \div 9 = \dfrac{\boxed{}}{\boxed{}}$

6 $2 \div 11 = \dfrac{\boxed{}}{\boxed{}}$

Rewrite each fraction as a division expression.

7 $\dfrac{7}{8} = $ _____ $\div$ _____

8 $\dfrac{5}{12} = $ _____ $\div$ _____

9 $\dfrac{1}{10} = $ _____ $\div$ _____

10 $\dfrac{6}{7} = $ _____ $\div$ _____

Fill in each blank.

11

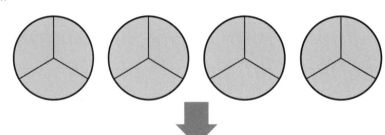

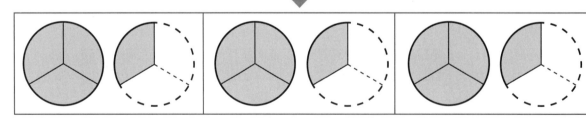

_____ $\div$ _____ $= \dfrac{\boxed{}}{\boxed{}}$

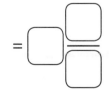

$= \boxed{}\dfrac{\boxed{}}{\boxed{}}$

12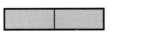

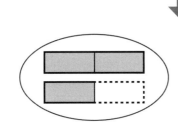 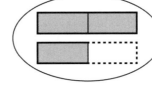

$$\underline{\hspace{2cm}} \div \underline{\hspace{2cm}} = \dfrac{\boxed{}}{\boxed{}}$$

$$= \boxed{} \dfrac{\boxed{}}{\boxed{}}$$

13 $7 \div 4 = \dfrac{\boxed{}}{\boxed{}}$

$$= \dfrac{\boxed{}}{\boxed{}} + \dfrac{\boxed{}}{\boxed{}}$$

$$= 1 + \dfrac{\boxed{}}{\boxed{}}$$

$$= \boxed{} \dfrac{\boxed{}}{\boxed{}}$$

14 $35 \div 11 = \dfrac{\boxed{}}{\boxed{}}$

$$= \dfrac{\boxed{}}{\boxed{}} + \dfrac{\boxed{}}{\boxed{}}$$

$$= 3 + \dfrac{\boxed{}}{\boxed{}}$$

$$= \boxed{} \dfrac{\boxed{}}{\boxed{}}$$

15 $18 \div 4 = \dfrac{\boxed{}}{\boxed{}}$

$= \dfrac{\boxed{}}{\boxed{}}$

$= \boxed{} \dfrac{\boxed{}}{\boxed{}}$

16 $22 \div 6 = \dfrac{\boxed{}}{\boxed{}}$

$= \dfrac{\boxed{}}{\boxed{}}$

$= \boxed{} \dfrac{\boxed{}}{\boxed{}}$

Rewrite each fraction as a division expression.

17 $\dfrac{5}{3} = $ _____ $\div$ _____

18 $\dfrac{7}{2} = $ _____ $\div$ _____

19 $\dfrac{9}{4} = $ _____ $\div$ _____

20 $\dfrac{18}{5} = $ _____ $\div$ _____

Solve.

21 5 pies were shared equally among 6 girls. What fraction of a pie did each girl receive? Explain.

_____

_____

_____

_____

Name: _____ Date: _____

Chapter 2 Extra Practice and Homework
Fractions and Mixed Numbers

Activity 2   Adding Unlike Fractions and Mixed Numbers

Shade and label each model to show the fractions. Then, find the sum.

 $\frac{1}{2}, \frac{1}{3}$

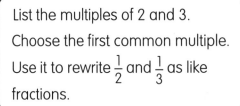
List the multiples of 2 and 3. Choose the first common multiple. Use it to rewrite $\frac{1}{2}$ and $\frac{1}{3}$ as like fractions.

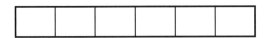

$\frac{1}{2} + \frac{1}{3} =$ _____ + _____

$=$ _____

 $\frac{1}{5}, \frac{1}{2}$

$\frac{1}{5} + \frac{1}{2} =$ _____ + _____

$=$ _____

3 $\frac{1}{6}, \frac{1}{4}$

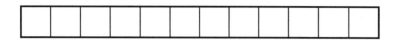

$\frac{1}{6} + \frac{1}{4} =$ _____ + _____

$=$ _____

4 $\frac{1}{5}, \frac{2}{3}$

$\frac{1}{5} + \frac{2}{3} =$ _____ + _____

$=$ _____

Look at the model. Write two addition equations.

$\frac{11}{12}$

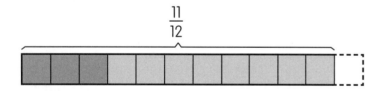

5 Addition equation 1:

$\dfrac{\boxed{}}{12} + \dfrac{\boxed{}}{12} = \dfrac{\boxed{}}{12}$

6 Addition equation 2 (fractions in simplest form):

_____ + _____ = _____

Add. Express each sum in simplest form.

7 $\dfrac{1}{3} + \dfrac{1}{9}$

8 $\dfrac{5}{8} + \dfrac{1}{2}$

9 $\dfrac{1}{2} + \dfrac{6}{7}$

10 $\dfrac{1}{3} + \dfrac{1}{5}$

Use benchmarks to estimate each sum.

11 $\dfrac{1}{3} + \dfrac{4}{7}$

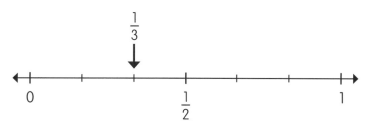

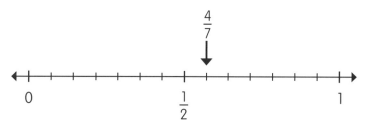

2 Adding Unlike Fractions and Mixed Numbers

12 $\frac{2}{3} + \frac{2}{9}$

13 $\frac{7}{9} + \frac{1}{7} + \frac{3}{5}$

Add.

14 $\frac{1}{2} + \frac{1}{3} + \frac{1}{4}$

Add. Express each sum in simplest form.

15 $3\frac{5}{8} + 2\frac{1}{4}$

$= 3\dfrac{\boxed{}}{\boxed{}} + 2\dfrac{\boxed{}}{\boxed{}}$

$= 5\dfrac{\boxed{}}{\boxed{}}$

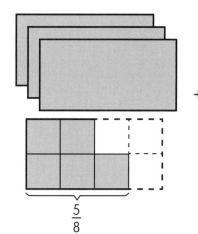

$\dfrac{5}{8}$ $+$ $\dfrac{1}{4}$

16 $1\frac{2}{3} + 2\frac{1}{4}$

$= 1\dfrac{\boxed{}}{\boxed{}} + 2\dfrac{\boxed{}}{\boxed{}}$

$= 3\dfrac{\boxed{}}{\boxed{}}$

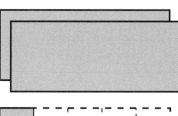
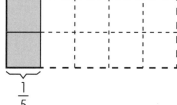

$\dfrac{2}{3}$ $+$ $\dfrac{1}{4}$

17 $2\frac{1}{5} + 3\frac{1}{2}$

$= 2\dfrac{\boxed{}}{\boxed{}} + 3\dfrac{\boxed{}}{\boxed{}}$

$= 5\dfrac{\boxed{}}{\boxed{}}$

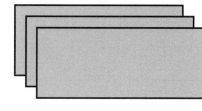
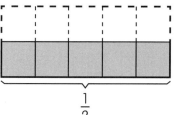

$\dfrac{1}{5}$ $+$ $\dfrac{1}{2}$

18 $3\frac{2}{7} + 2\frac{5}{14}$

19 $5\frac{7}{12} + 3\frac{1}{4}$

20 $4\frac{1}{15} + 1\frac{3}{10}$

21 $12\frac{1}{9} + 9\frac{5}{6}$

22 $1\frac{4}{5} + 2\frac{1}{3}$

$= 1\dfrac{\boxed{}}{\boxed{}} + 2\dfrac{\boxed{}}{\boxed{}}$

$= 3\dfrac{\boxed{}}{\boxed{}}$

$= 4\dfrac{\boxed{}}{\boxed{}}$

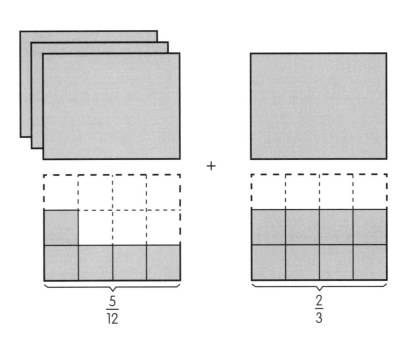

$+$

$\dfrac{4}{5}$ $\qquad$ $\dfrac{1}{3}$

23 $3\frac{5}{12} + 1\frac{2}{3}$

$= 3\dfrac{\boxed{}}{\boxed{}} + 1\dfrac{\boxed{}}{\boxed{}}$

$= 4\dfrac{\boxed{}}{\boxed{}}$

$= 5\dfrac{\boxed{}}{\boxed{}}$

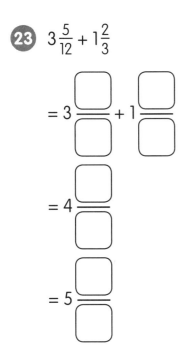

$+$

$\dfrac{5}{12}$ $\qquad$ $\dfrac{2}{3}$

24 $2\frac{3}{4} + 3\frac{2}{5}$

25 $2\frac{5}{9} + 1\frac{5}{6}$

26 $7\frac{8}{9} + 9\frac{5}{12}$

27 $5\frac{7}{12} + 1\frac{3}{4}$

Use benchmarks to estimate each sum.

28 $6\frac{3}{5} + 4\frac{5}{6}$

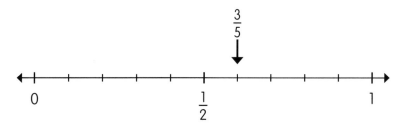

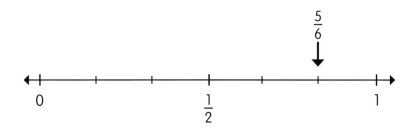

29 $9\frac{6}{7} + 7\frac{5}{12}$

30 $4\frac{7}{12} + 10\frac{1}{9}$

Solve.

31 Show $3\frac{1}{4} + 1\frac{1}{2}$ on the number line.

Chapter 2

Extra Practice and Homework
Fractions and Mixed Numbers

Activity 3 Subtracting Unlike Fractions and Mixed Numbers

Rewrite each pair of fractions as like fractions and find the difference.

 1

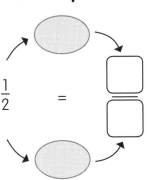

$\dfrac{1}{2} =$

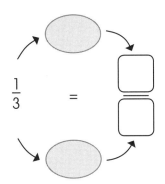

$\dfrac{1}{3} =$

What is the first common multiple of 2 and 3?

$\dfrac{1}{2} = \boxed{}$

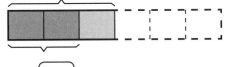

$\dfrac{1}{3} = \boxed{}$

$\dfrac{1}{2} - \dfrac{1}{3} = $ _____ $-$ _____

$= $ _____

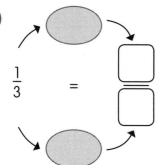

$$\frac{1}{3} = \boxed{}$$

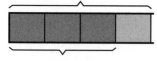

$$\frac{1}{4} = \boxed{}$$

$$\frac{1}{3} - \frac{1}{4} = \underline{} - \underline{}$$

$$= \underline{}$$

Subtract. Express each difference in simplest form.

3 $\dfrac{7}{12} - \dfrac{1}{2}$

4 $\dfrac{4}{5} - \dfrac{1}{3}$

5 $\dfrac{7}{9} - \dfrac{1}{6}$

6 $1 - \dfrac{5}{6} - \dfrac{1}{12}$

Use benchmarks to estimate each difference.

7 $\frac{4}{5} - \frac{3}{8}$

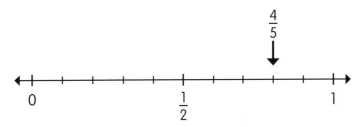

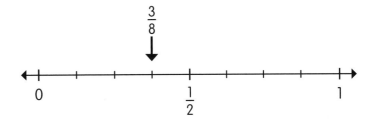

8 $\frac{9}{10} - \frac{1}{6}$

9 $\frac{5}{12} - \frac{1}{9}$

Solve.

10 Dylan drew a model to find $\frac{4}{5} - \frac{1}{2}$. His model is drawn incorrectly. Explain his mistakes. Then, draw the correct model and find the difference.

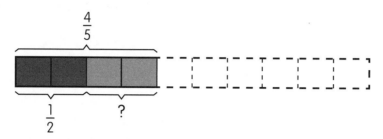

Dylan's model is wrong because:

The correct model is:

Subtract. Express each difference in simplest form.

 11 $3\frac{2}{3} - \frac{5}{12}$

$= 3\dfrac{\boxed{}}{\boxed{}} - \dfrac{5}{12}$

$= 3\dfrac{\boxed{}}{\boxed{}}$

$= 3\dfrac{\boxed{}}{\boxed{}}$

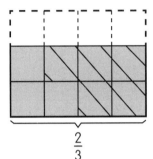

$\frac{2}{3}$

12 $4\frac{8}{9} - 3\frac{1}{3}$

$= 4\dfrac{8}{9} - 3\dfrac{\boxed{}}{\boxed{}}$

$= 1\dfrac{\boxed{}}{\boxed{}}$

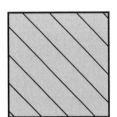
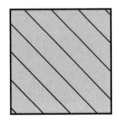
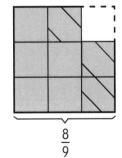

$\frac{8}{9}$

13 $3\frac{7}{12} - 2\frac{3}{8}$

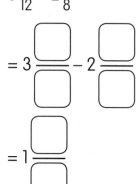

$= 3\dfrac{\boxed{}}{\boxed{}} - 2\dfrac{\boxed{}}{\boxed{}}$

$= 1\dfrac{\boxed{}}{\boxed{}}$

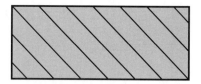
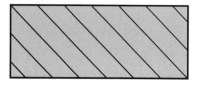
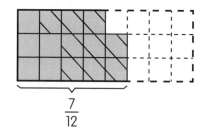

$\dfrac{7}{12}$

14 $3\frac{5}{9} - 1\frac{1}{2}$

15 $7\frac{5}{6} - 2\frac{1}{4}$

16 $3\frac{1}{4} - 1\frac{7}{8}$

$= 3\dfrac{\boxed{}}{\boxed{}} - 1\frac{7}{8}$

$= \boxed{}\dfrac{\boxed{}}{\boxed{}} - \boxed{}\dfrac{\boxed{}}{\boxed{}}$

$= \boxed{}\dfrac{\boxed{}}{\boxed{}}$

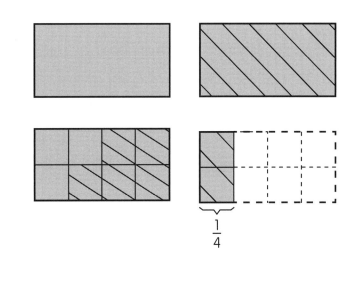

$\underbrace{\qquad}_{\frac{1}{4}}$

17 $5\frac{1}{3} - 3\frac{5}{12}$

$= 5\dfrac{\boxed{}}{\boxed{}} - 3\frac{5}{12}$

$= \boxed{}\dfrac{\boxed{}}{\boxed{}} - \boxed{}\dfrac{\boxed{}}{\boxed{}}$

$= \boxed{}\dfrac{\boxed{}}{\boxed{}}$

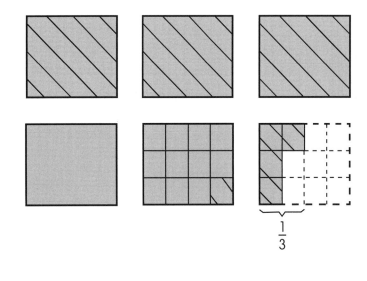

$\underbrace{\qquad}_{\frac{1}{3}}$

18 $4\frac{1}{5} - 1\frac{1}{3}$

19 $6\frac{3}{8} - 3\frac{5}{6}$

20 $7\frac{1}{4} - 5\frac{11}{12}$

21 $8\frac{1}{3} - 4\frac{3}{4}$

Solve.

22 $2\frac{1}{2} - $ _____ $= \frac{4}{5}$

23 $6 - $ _____ $= 3\frac{2}{5}$

Use benchmarks to estimate each difference.

24 $7\frac{2}{9} - 6\frac{5}{12}$

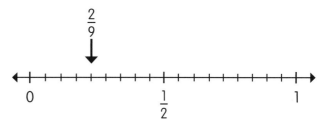

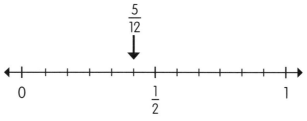

25 $12\frac{2}{5} - 8\frac{7}{12}$

26 $20\frac{1}{8} - 5\frac{1}{3}$

Chapter 2

Extra Practice and Homework
Fractions and Mixed Numbers

Activity 4   Real-World Problems: Fractions and Mixed Numbers

Solve. Show your work. Draw a bar model to help you.

1 José puts an empty container under a leaking faucet. $\frac{3}{8}$ quart of water collects inside the container in the first hour. $\frac{1}{6}$ quart of water collects inside the container in the second hour. How much water collects in the container in the two hours?

2 Ms. Mackenzie buys $\frac{8}{9}$ pound of meat. She uses $\frac{3}{4}$ pound of the meat to make meatballs. How many pounds of meat are left?

3 An earthworm is at the bottom of a well. The earthworm climbs $70\frac{3}{5}$ inches in the first six minutes. It climbs $64\frac{1}{3}$ inches in the next six minutes. How far is the earthworm from the bottom of the well after 12 minutes?

4 Jack is jogging along a track. He has already jogged $1\frac{2}{3}$ miles. He plans to jog a total of $3\frac{1}{4}$ miles. How many miles does he have left to jog?

5 Ms. Lopez buys 1 quart of milk. Luis drinks $\frac{2}{7}$ quart of it. Maite drinks $\frac{1}{3}$ quart of it. How many quarts of milk are left?

6 An organic farmer buys a piece of land. She plants tomatoes on $\frac{5}{9}$ of the land and green beans on $\frac{1}{12}$ of the land. She plants potatoes on the remaining piece of land. What fraction of the land does she plant with potatoes?

7 A paper bag contains three types of bagels — plain, wholewheat, and sesame. The weight of the plain bagels is $1\frac{2}{3}$ pounds. The weight of the wholewheat bagels is $2\frac{5}{6}$ pounds. The total weight of the three types of bagels is 5 pounds. What is the weight of the sesame bagels?

8 Kyle and Trinity go for a walk every morning. Kyle walks $2\frac{1}{4}$ miles. Trinity walks $1\frac{3}{8}$ miles less than Kyle. What is the total distance they walk every morning?

9 Anna uses $\frac{3}{4}$ gallon of paint to paint her room. Jessica uses $\frac{4}{5}$ gallon more paint than Anna to paint her room. How many gallons of paint do they use altogether?

10 A monkey climbs $3\frac{3}{5}$ feet up a coconut tree that has a height of 10 feet. It rests for a while and continues to climb another $4\frac{2}{3}$ feet up the tree. How many more feet must the monkey climb to reach the top of the tree?

1 **Mathematical Habit 4** **Use mathematical models**

Explain how $\frac{2}{3}$ and $2 \div 3$ are related. Draw models to help you.

2 **Mathematical Habit 4** Use mathematical models

$$\frac{1}{8} + \frac{2}{3} = ?$$

Draw a model, and show the steps you can use to add $\frac{2}{3}$ to $\frac{1}{8}$.

1 Mathematical Habit **6** Use precise mathematical language

Use the digits 2, 3, 4, 5, and 6 only once to fill in each blank to form the greatest possible difference.

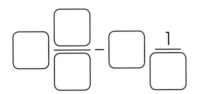

2 Mathematical Habit **6** Use precise mathematical language

The $\boxed{3}$ key on your calculator is not working. Show two other ways you can use the calculator to find the sum of $2\frac{5}{6}$ and $1\frac{3}{4}$.

3 | **Mathematical Habit** **4** **Use mathematical models**

Ms. Davis mixes cement with sand. She uses $3\frac{3}{4}$ kilograms of cement and $\frac{1}{2}$ kilogram more sand than cement. She needs 10 kilograms of the mixture. Does she have enough mixture? If yes, how much more does she have?

If no, how much more does she need?

SCHOOL-to-HOME
CONNECTIONS

Chapter 3

Multiplying and Dividing Fractions and Mixed Numbers

Dear Family,

In this chapter, your child will learn to multiply and divide fractions and mixed numbers. Skills your child will practice include:

- multiplying proper and improper fractions by whole numbers
- multiplying proper fractions
- multiplying improper fractions
- multiplying mixed numbers and whole numbers
- dividing unit and proper fractions by whole numbers, and vice versa
- solving real-world problems

Math Practice

Whether we are building, repairing, cooking, or working with money, we frequently find the need to work with fractions. At the end of this chapter, you may want to carry out these activities with your child. These activities will help to strengthen your child's understanding of multiplying and dividing fractions and mixed numbers.

Activity 1

- Take turns rolling a number cube to get four numbers.
- Have your child write two proper or improper fractions using the numbers.
- Ask your child to multiply the fractions.
- Repeat the activity several times.

Activity 2

- Ask your child to roll a number cube to get a number, for example, 3.
- Have your child divide the number by a unit fraction, for example, $3 \div \frac{1}{2} = 6$.
- Have your child divide the unit fraction by the number, for example, $\frac{1}{2} \div 3 = \frac{1}{6}$.
- Ask your child: "What do you notice about the quotients?" ($\frac{1}{6}$ is the reciprocal of 6.)
- Repeat the activity using another unit fraction, for example, $\frac{1}{4}$.

Math Talk

Use the following examples to discuss multiplication and division involving fractions and mixed numbers.

$$\frac{2}{3} \times \frac{5}{6} = \frac{2 \times 5}{3 \times 6}$$
$$= \frac{10}{18}$$
$$= \frac{5}{9}$$

$$3\frac{1}{2} \times 4 = \frac{7}{\cancel{2}_1} \times \cancel{4}^2$$
$$= 14$$

$$\frac{1}{3} \div 4 = \frac{1}{3} \times \frac{1}{4}$$
$$= \frac{1}{12}$$

Encourage your child to write and solve a multiplication or division problem involving fractions or mixed numbers.

SCHOOL
TO HOME

BLANK

Name: _____ Date: _____

Activity 1   Multiplying Fractions and Whole Numbers

Fill in each blank.

1 $\frac{1}{2}$ of $18 = \frac{1}{2} \times \boxed{}$

$= \dfrac{1 \times \boxed{}}{2}$

$= \dfrac{\boxed{}}{2}$

$= \boxed{}$

2 $\frac{1}{4}$ of $28 =$ _____

3 $\frac{3}{5}$ of $40 =$ _____

4 $\frac{4}{7}$ of $49 =$ _____

5 $\frac{5}{8}$ of $64 =$ _____

Find each product.

6 $\frac{5}{4}$ of 28 = _____

7 $\frac{9}{5}$ of 45 = _____

8 $\frac{7}{6}$ of 18 = _____

9 $\frac{10}{3} \times 21$ = _____

10 $\frac{7}{4} \times 24$ = _____

11 $35 \times \frac{8}{7}$ = _____

Extra Practice and Homework Grade 5A

Chapter 3

Extra Practice and Homework
Multiplying and Dividing Fractions and Mixed Numbers

Activity 2 Multiplying Proper Fractions

Fill in each blank.

1

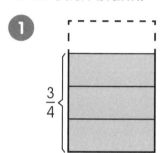 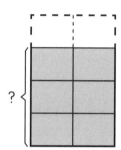

$\dfrac{1}{2}$ of $\dfrac{3}{4}$ = $\dfrac{\square}{\square}$ × $\dfrac{\square}{\square}$

= $\dfrac{\square}{\square}$

Draw a model to find each product.

2 $\dfrac{3}{8} \times \dfrac{1}{2}$

3 $\dfrac{5}{12} \times \dfrac{7}{8}$

4 $\dfrac{2}{11} \times \dfrac{7}{12}$

5 $\dfrac{3}{8} \times \dfrac{4}{9}$

Fill in each blank.

6 $\dfrac{1}{3} \times \dfrac{5}{8} = \dfrac{\boxed{}}{\boxed{}} \times \dfrac{\boxed{}}{\boxed{}}$

$= \dfrac{\boxed{}}{\boxed{}}$

7 $\dfrac{2}{7} \times \dfrac{9}{11} = \dfrac{\boxed{}}{\boxed{}} \times \dfrac{\boxed{}}{\boxed{}}$

$= \dfrac{\boxed{}}{\boxed{}}$

8 $\dfrac{2}{5} \times \dfrac{7}{10} = \dfrac{\boxed{}}{\boxed{}} \times \dfrac{\boxed{}}{\boxed{}}$

$= \dfrac{1}{\boxed{}} \times \dfrac{\boxed{}}{\boxed{}}$

$= \dfrac{1 \times \boxed{}}{\boxed{} \times \boxed{}}$

$= \dfrac{\boxed{}}{\boxed{}}$

9 $\dfrac{3}{4} \times \dfrac{8}{9} = \dfrac{\boxed{}}{\boxed{}} \times \dfrac{\boxed{}}{\boxed{}}$

$= \dfrac{1}{\boxed{}} \times \dfrac{\boxed{}}{\boxed{}}$

$= \dfrac{1}{1} \times \dfrac{\boxed{}}{\boxed{}}$

$= \dfrac{\boxed{}}{\boxed{}}$

Solve.

10 a

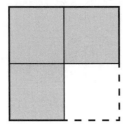

b

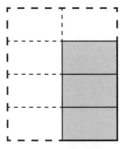

c

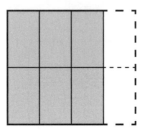

Which of the above shows $\frac{3}{4}$ of $\frac{1}{2}$? _____

11 Shade part of the rectangle to show $\frac{2}{5}$ of $\frac{1}{3}$.

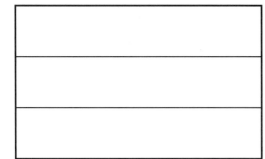

Chapter 3

Extra Practice and Homework
Multiplying and Dividing Fractions and Mixed Numbers

Activity 3 Real-World Problems: Multiplying Proper Fractions

Solve. Draw a bar model to help you. Express each answer in simplest form.

1 Ms. Clark has some eggs in the refrigerator. She takes out $\frac{3}{5}$ of the eggs to make waffles and scrambled eggs. She uses $\frac{2}{3}$ of the eggs she took out to make waffles. What fraction of the total number of eggs does Ms. Clark use to make waffles?

2 Mr. Reyes has $\frac{5}{6}$ yard of lace. He uses $\frac{4}{5}$ of it for trimming a dress for his daughter, and the rest for a jewel box. How much lace does he use for the jewel box?

3. Lily finished a task in $\frac{3}{4}$ hour. Ella finished it in $\frac{4}{5}$ of the time Lily took. How long did Ella take to finish the task?

4. Ava has a bottle containing $\frac{7}{8}$ quart of milk. She pours $\frac{4}{5}$ of it into a bowl. What amount of milk does she pour into the bowl?

5. Aidan ran $\frac{3}{4}$ mile in a race. Bryan ran $\frac{2}{5}$ of the distance that Aidan ran. What distance did Bryan run?

6 Ms. Brown spends $\frac{1}{6}$ of her paycheck and saves $\frac{2}{5}$ of the remaining amount. What fraction of her total paycheck is saved?

7 $\frac{3}{4}$ of the members in Ian's family wear glasses. $\frac{1}{3}$ of those who do **not** wear glasses are male. What fraction of the family are males who do **not** wear glasses?

8 Diego folded a set of origami figures. $\frac{5}{8}$ of this set are cranes and $\frac{1}{6}$ of the remainder are frogs. The rest are grasshoppers. What fraction of the origami figures are grasshoppers?

9 $\frac{2}{3}$ of the flowers in a garden are roses. $\frac{5}{12}$ of the roses in the garden are yellow and the rest are red. What fraction of the flowers are red roses?

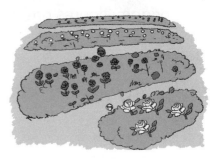

10 Silvana collects local and foreign coins. $\frac{1}{4}$ of the coins in her collection are foreign coins. $\frac{2}{5}$ of the foreign coins are from Mexico. What fraction of the collection are foreign coins that are **not** from Mexico?

Chapter 3

Extra Practice and Homework
Multiplying and Dividing Fractions and Mixed Numbers

Activity 4   Multiplying Improper Fractions

Fill in each blank.

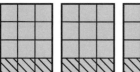

$$\frac{8}{3} \times \frac{1}{4} = \frac{\boxed{} \times \boxed{}}{\boxed{} \times \boxed{}} = \frac{\boxed{}}{\boxed{}} = \frac{\boxed{}}{\boxed{}}$$

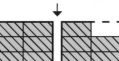

$$\frac{11}{2} \times \frac{1}{3} = \frac{\boxed{} \times \boxed{}}{\boxed{} \times \boxed{}} = \frac{\boxed{}}{\boxed{}} = \boxed{} \frac{\boxed{}}{\boxed{}}$$

Multiply. Express each product in simplest form.

3 $\dfrac{7}{4} \times \dfrac{1}{3}$

4 $\dfrac{9}{8} \times \dfrac{2}{7}$

5 $\dfrac{4}{5} \times \dfrac{7}{6}$

6 $\dfrac{2}{5} \times \dfrac{15}{7}$

7 $\dfrac{8}{3} \times \dfrac{3}{10}$

8 $\dfrac{5}{3} \times \dfrac{3}{20}$

9 $\dfrac{3}{4} \times \dfrac{16}{9}$

10 $\dfrac{2}{5} \times \dfrac{15}{4}$

11 $\frac{16}{7} \times \frac{3}{4}$

12 $\frac{7}{8} \times \frac{6}{5}$

13 $\frac{11}{12} \times \frac{28}{3}$

14 $\frac{16}{7} \times \frac{21}{2}$

15 $\frac{25}{12} \times \frac{8}{5}$

16 $\frac{32}{9} \times \frac{45}{16}$

17 $\frac{21}{5} \times \frac{15}{6}$

18 $\frac{25}{4} \times \frac{9}{5}$

19 $\dfrac{10}{3} \times \dfrac{7}{2}$

20 $\dfrac{21}{12} \times \dfrac{5}{3}$

Solve.

21 Which of the following expressions have the same results?

a $\quad \dfrac{3}{2} \times \dfrac{1}{5}$

b $\quad \dfrac{3}{7} \times \dfrac{7}{10}$

c $\quad \dfrac{4}{3} \times \dfrac{1}{3}$

Chapter 3

Extra Practice and Homework
Multiplying and Dividing Fractions and Mixed Numbers

Activity 5   Multiplying Mixed Numbers and Whole Numbers

Fill in each blank.

1

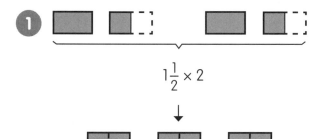

$$1\frac{1}{2} \times 2$$

$$1\frac{1}{2} \times 2 = \frac{\boxed{}}{\boxed{}} \times \boxed{} = \boxed{}$$

2

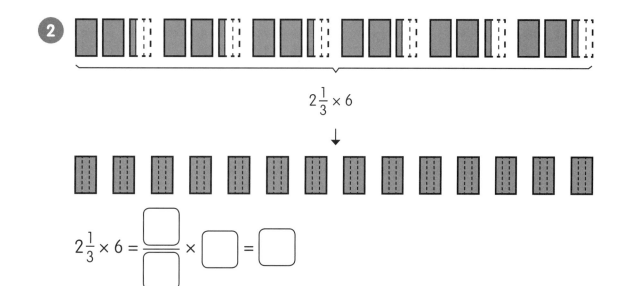

$$2\frac{1}{3} \times 6$$

$$2\frac{1}{3} \times 6 = \frac{\boxed{}}{\boxed{}} \times \boxed{} = \boxed{}$$

Multiply. Express each product in simplest form.

3 $9 \times 2\frac{1}{3} =$ _____

4 $8 \times 3\frac{3}{4} =$ _____

5 $4\frac{1}{5} \times 15 =$ _____

6 $2\frac{3}{7} \times 28 =$ _____

7 $24 \times 1\frac{5}{6} =$ _____

8 $4\frac{1}{2} \times 18 =$ _____

9 $2\frac{3}{4} \times 16 = $ _____

10 $32 \times 3\frac{1}{8} = $ _____

11 $6 \times 2\frac{1}{5} = $ _____

12 $3 \times 3\frac{5}{8} = $ _____

13 $4 \times 2\frac{7}{9} = $ _____

14 $5 \times 2\frac{3}{7} = $ _____

15 $2\frac{1}{4} \times 7 =$ _____

16 $1\frac{4}{5} \times 12 =$ _____

17 $12 \times 2\frac{3}{8} =$ _____

18 $26 \times 1\frac{1}{6} =$ _____

Solve.

19 Is the product of 6 and $10\frac{1}{4}$ greater than or less than each of its factors? Explain your reasoning.

20 Is the product of $4\frac{2}{5}$ and $5\frac{3}{4}$ greater than or less than $4\frac{2}{5}$? Is it greater than or less than $5\frac{3}{4}$? Explain your reasoning.

Shade square tiles to multiply each pair of mixed numbers. Express each product in simplest form.

21 $1\frac{1}{2} \times 2\frac{1}{3}$

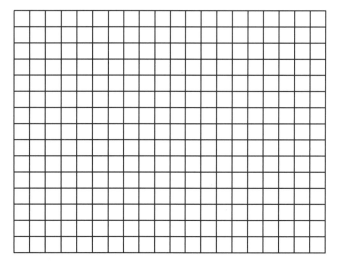

22 $1\frac{5}{6} \times 2\frac{2}{3}$

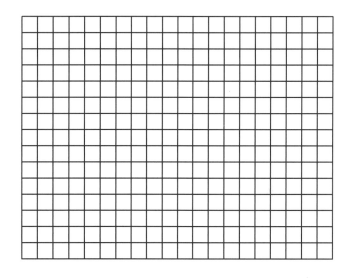

23 $2\frac{1}{6} \times 2\frac{1}{2}$

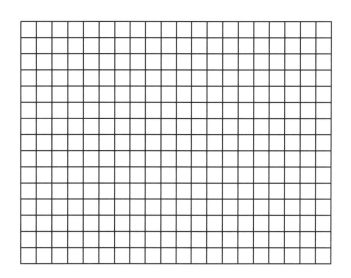

Draw an area model to multiply each pair of mixed numbers. Express each product in simplest form.

24 $1\frac{3}{5} \times 1\frac{4}{7}$

25 $2\frac{1}{6} \times 3\frac{1}{4}$

26 $3\frac{1}{5} \times 4\frac{2}{3}$

Extra Practice and Homework Grade 5A

Name: _____ Date: _____

Extra Practice and Homework
Multiplying and Dividing Fractions and Mixed Numbers

Activity 6 Real-World Problems: Multiplying Mixed Numbers

Solve. Show your work.

1 There are 8 guests at a party. Each guest eats $2\frac{1}{4}$ oranges. How many oranges do the guests eat in all?

1 guest ⟶ $2\frac{1}{4}$ oranges

8 guests ⟶ _____ × _____

= _____ oranges

The guests eat _____ oranges in all.

2 One pound of chicken costs \$4. Zachary buys $8\frac{1}{2}$ pounds of chicken. How much does Zachary pay for the chicken?

3 Timothy practices the piano for $1\frac{2}{5}$ hours each every Saturday and Sunday. How long does he practice over the two days? Express your answer in hours and minutes.

4 Ms. Perez buys 5 pieces of fabric. Each piece of fabric is $1\frac{7}{10}$ yards long.

a What is the total length of the fabric she buys?

b One yard of the fabric costs $5. How much does she pay for all the fabric?

5 Molly works $1\frac{1}{2}$ hours a day and is paid $7 per hour. She works 5 days a week. How much does Molly earn in a week?

Chapter 3

Extra Practice and Homework
Multiplying and Dividing Fractions and Mixed Numbers

Activity 7   Dividing Fractions and Whole Numbers

Shade parts of each model to show the division expression. Then, fill in each blank.

1 $\frac{1}{3} \div 2$

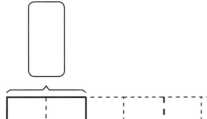

 is shaded.

$\frac{1}{3} \div 2 = $ _____

2 $\frac{1}{6} \div 3$

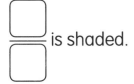 is shaded.

$\frac{1}{6} \div 3 = $ _____

Divide. Express each quotient in simplest form. Draw models to help you.

3 $\frac{4}{5} \div 2$

4 $\frac{6}{7} \div 3$

5 $\frac{3}{4} \div 2$

6 $\frac{2}{5} \div 3$

Divide. Express each quotient in simplest form.

7 $\frac{4}{5} \div 7$

8 $\frac{5}{8} \div 9$

9 $\frac{8}{9} \div 4$

10 $\frac{10}{11} \div 5$

Divide. Draw a model to help you.

11 $1 \div \frac{1}{4} =$ _____

12 $3 \div \frac{1}{3} =$ _____

13 $3 \div \frac{1}{5} =$ _____

14 $5 \div \frac{1}{8} =$ _____

15 $9 \div \frac{1}{6} =$ _____

Solve. Draw a model to help you. Express each answer in simplest form.

16 Ms. Price's garden covers $\frac{2}{5}$ of an acre of land. She divides the garden into 4 equal sections. What fraction of an acre is each section of the garden?

17 Sebastian pours $\frac{4}{9}$ quart of milk from a pitcher equally into 4 mugs.

    a   Find the amount of milk in each mug.

    b   Find the amount of milk in 3 mugs.

18 Mr. Smith buys $\frac{3}{5}$ pound of meat. He divides the meat into 6 equal portions.

    a Find the weight of 1 portion of meat.

    b Find the weight of 4 portions of meat.

19 Mr. Turner buys a piece of land with an area of $\frac{5}{6}$ square kilometer. He divides the land equally into 4 small plots. What is the total area of 3 of the small plots of land?

20 Sara has a 5-foot piece of canvas. She cuts the canvas into shorter pieces that are $\frac{1}{4}$ feet long. How many shorter pieces will she have?

21 Ethan uses $\frac{1}{4}$ of the water in a full bucket to water 1 potted plant. How many potted plants can Ethan water with 3 of these buckets of water?

22 Ms. Patel needs $\frac{2}{3}$ meter of cloth to make a pillow case. What is the most number of pillow cases that she can make with 5 meters of cloth?

Chapter 3

Extra Practice and Homework
Multiplying and Dividing Fractions and Mixed Numbers

Activity 8 Real-World Problems: Multiplying and Dividing with Fractions

Solve. Show your work. Draw a bar model to help you.

1 Dominic typed 72 pages of notes one day. He typed $\frac{1}{2}$ of the pages in the morning and $\frac{1}{3}$ of the pages in the afternoon. He typed the rest of the pages in the evening. How many pages of notes did he type in the morning and afternoon?

2 Trevon spent 6 hours playing games, studying, and talking with his friends last Saturday. He spent $\frac{2}{5}$ of the time playing games and $\frac{1}{2}$ of the time studying. How many minutes did he spend talking with his friends?

3 Ms. Young earns $720 a week. She spends $\frac{1}{3}$ of her money on groceries and household goods, and $\frac{3}{4}$ of the remaining money on clothes. How much money does she spend altogether on groceries, household goods, and clothes?

4 Alyssa takes part in a triathlon. She cycles $\frac{4}{5}$ of the route, runs $\frac{7}{8}$ of the remaining route, and swims the rest of the route. She swims 0.9 mile. Find the total distance of the triathlon route.

5 Ms. Evans has a 2-pound package of flour. She uses $\frac{2}{5}$ of the flour to make a pie. She then uses $\frac{3}{10}$ of the remaining flour to make bread. Find the weight of the package of flour that she has left. Express your answer as a decimal.

6 Daniel collects $\frac{6}{7}$ quart of rainwater. He uses $\frac{1}{2}$ of the water to clean his bicycle and uses the remaining water equally for 3 houseplants. What volume of water does he use for each houseplant?

7 Chloe spends $\frac{8}{9}$ hour reading the newspaper. She spends $\frac{1}{4}$ of the time reading the world news, and splits the remaining time equally between the sports news and the comics. How much time does she spend reading the comics?

8 A square foot of wall space needs $\frac{1}{8}$ quart of paint. Uriah has 7 quarts of paint. He uses 2 quarts to paint a pipe. How many square feet of wall can he paint with the rest of the paint?

9 Antonio spends $\frac{1}{6}$ hour making one friendship bracelet. He spends 3 hours before lunch and 2 hours after lunch making some bracelets. How many bracelets does he make in all?

10 Grace spends half her time practicing her drums, and $\frac{3}{4}$ of the remaining time on homework and dinner after school one afternoon. She spends the remaining $\frac{3}{4}$ hour reading. How long does she practice the drums?

11 Ana spends $\frac{5}{9}$ of her vacation at summer camp. She spends $\frac{3}{4}$ of the remaining time at her grandparent's home. She spends the remaining 7 days holidaying with her family. How many days of summer vacation does she get each summer?

Mathematical Habit 2 **Use mathematical reasoning**

Hannah drew a model to solve the following problem:

Wyatt pours $\frac{1}{3}$ of a bottle of juice into his glass. Sean pours $\frac{1}{3}$ of the remainder into his glass. What fraction of the bottle of juice is left?

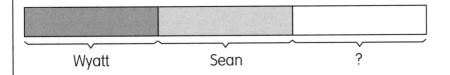

$$1 - \frac{1}{3} - \frac{1}{3} = \frac{1}{3}$$

$\frac{1}{3}$ of the bottle of juice is left.

Did Hannah solve the problem correctly? Explain. Show the correct work.

Mathematical Habit 4 Use mathematical models

June's Market sold 24 heads of lettuce one morning. $\frac{2}{7}$ of the remaining heads of lettuce were sold that afternoon. The number of heads of lettuce left was now $\frac{1}{2}$ of the number the market had at the beginning of the day. How many heads of lettuce were there at the beginning of the day?

SCHOOL-to-HOME
CONNECTIONS

Chapter 4

Decimals

Dear Family,
In this chapter, your child will learn about decimals. Skills your child will practice include:
- reading and writing thousandths in decimal and fractional form
- comparing, ordering, and rounding decimals
- rewriting decimals as fractions and mixed numbers, and vice versa

Math Practice
Rounding decimals to a specific place is a helpful skill to have. We often round decimals to estimate measurements and costs. At the end of this chapter, you may want to carry out this activity with your child. This activity will help to strengthen your child's understanding of decimals.

Activity
- Prepare a place-value chart as shown.

Ones	.	Tenths	Hundredths	Thousandths
	.			
	.			
	.			
	.			
	.			
	.			

- Take turns rolling the number cube to get four numbers.
- Write each number in each place.
- Ask your child to read the decimal aloud.
- Have your child round the decimal to the nearest hundredth, then to the nearest tenth and lastly, to the nearest whole number.
- Ask your child to rewrite the decimal as a fraction or mixed number.
- Repeat the activity several times.

 Math Talk

Have your child read the values in the following place-value chart and write the **decimals**.

Ones	.	Tenths	Hundredths	Thousandths
2	.	1	3	4
4	.	0	5	5
3	.	9	2	1

(2.134; 4.055; 3.921)

Help your child understand that the fraction $\frac{1}{1,000}$ and the decimal 0.001 are equivalent. Use this understanding to discuss how to rewrite the decimals in the chart as **mixed numbers**.
$(2\frac{134}{1,000}; 4\frac{55}{1,000}; 3\frac{921}{1,000})$

Use the following examples to discuss how to round decimals to the nearest tenth and to the nearest hundredth.

10.946 is 10.9 when **rounded to the nearest tenth**.
10.946 is 10.95 when **rounded to the nearest hundredth**.

Encourage your child to write and explain more examples of rounding decimals to the nearest tenth and to the nearest hundredth.

BLANK

Chapter 4 Extra Practice and Homework Decimals

Activity 1   Understanding Thousandths

Write each decimal shown.

1. 0.1 0.01 0.001 0.001
   0.1 0.01 0.001 0.001
   0.01 0.001
   0.001
   0.001   _____

2. 1 0.01 0.001
   1 0.01 0.001
   1 0.01 0.001
   1 0.01 0.001
   0.01 0.001   _____

3. 1 1 0.001 0.001
   1 0.001 0.001
   1 0.001 0.001
   1 0.001 0.001
   1 0.001   _____

_____

Express each of the following as a decimal.

5 7 thousandths = _____

6 19 thousandths = _____

7 235 thousandths = _____

8 300 thousandths = _____

9 $\dfrac{13}{1,000}$ = _____

10 $\dfrac{55}{1,000}$ = _____

11 $\dfrac{228}{1,000}$ = _____

12 $\dfrac{430}{1,000}$ = _____

13 $2\dfrac{3}{1,000}$ = _____

14 $6\dfrac{61}{1,000}$ = _____

15 $7\dfrac{107}{1,000}$ = _____

16 $8\dfrac{240}{1,000}$ = _____

17 $\dfrac{1,005}{1,000}$ = _____

18 $\dfrac{1,013}{1,000}$ = _____

19 $\dfrac{2,341}{1,000}$ = _____

20 $\dfrac{3,450}{1,000}$ = _____

Fill in each blank.

21 4 hundredths = _____ thousandths

22 8 tenths 5 hundredths = _____ thousandths

Extra Practice and Homework Grade 5A

23 20 thousandths = _____ hundredths

24 125 thousandths = 1 tenth _____ thousandths

25 0.126 = 1 tenth 2 hundredths _____ thousandths

26 0.352 = 3 tenths _____ hundredths 2 thousandths

27 0.014 = _____ thousandths

28 0.178 = _____ thousandths

29 0.76 = _____ thousandths

30 1.035 = 1 one and _____ thousandths

Mark an X to show where each decimal is located.

31 0.006   **32** 0.024   **33** 0.033

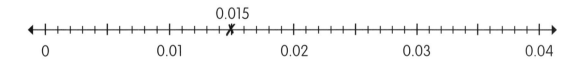

Find the decimal that each labeled point represents.

34

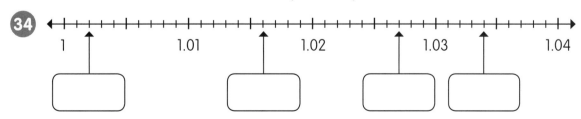

Fill in each blank.

In 5.074

35 the digit 4 is in the _____ place.

36 the value of the digit 7 is _____.

37 the digit 0 is in the _____ place.

38 the digit 5 stands for _____.

9.876 can be written in expanded form as 9 + 0.8 + 0.07 + 0.006. Write each decimal in expanded form.

39 6.426 = _____ + _____ + _____ + _____

40 3.642 = _____ + _____ + _____ + _____

1.234 can be written in expanded form as $1 + \frac{2}{10} + \frac{3}{100} + \frac{4}{1,000}$**. Write each decimal in expanded form.**

41 4.153 = ⬜ + ⬜ + ⬜ + ⬜

42 8.381 = ⬜ + ⬜ + ⬜ + ⬜

Fill in each blank.

43 Write a decimal with the digit 6 in the tenths place. _____

44 In 4.⬜97, the digit in ⬜ is $\frac{1}{3}$ of the digit in the hundredths place.

What is the digit in the tenths place? _____

Extra Practice and Homework
Decimals

Activity 2 Comparing, Ordering, and Rounding Decimals

Compare each pair of decimals. Fill in each blank. Write > or < in each ◯.

1

Ones	.	Tenths	Hundredths	Thousandths
0	.	0	2	
0	.	0	1	5

_____ is greater than _____.

_____ ◯ _____

2

Ones	.	Tenths	Hundredths	Thousandths
0	.	3	0	8
0	.	2	9	

_____ is less than _____.

_____ ◯ _____

3

Ones	.	Tenths	Hundredths	Thousandths
4	.	0	9	1
4	.	1	9	

_____ is less than _____.

_____ ◯ _____

Compare each pair of decimals. Write the greater decimal.

4 11.6 or 21.8 _____

5 10.55 or 10.05 _____

6 20.07 or 20.01 _____

7 100.202 or 100.212 _____

Write >, <, or =.

8 3.7 ◯ 0.370

9 0.150 ◯ 0.51

10 0.205 ◯ 2.05

11 2.3 ◯ 2.30

Compare each set of decimals. Circle the greatest decimal and underline the least.

12 1.03, 1.3, 0.13

13 0.5, 0.53, 0.503

14 2.35, 2.305, 2.035

15 8.7, 8.07, 8.701

Order the decimals in each set from least to greatest.

16 3.33, 3.03, 3.303 _____

17 5.51, 5.051, 5.501 _____

18 4, 4.01, 4.001 _____

19 0.023, 0.203, 0.230 _____

Write the missing decimal in each blank. Mark an X to show where each given decimal is located. Round each given decimal to the nearest hundredth.

20

1.056 rounded to the nearest hundredth is _____.

21

2.395 rounded to the nearest hundredth is _____.

22

5.994 rounded to the nearest hundredth is _____.

Fill in each blank.

23 The mass of a sewing needle is 0.585 gram.
Round the mass to the nearest hundredth of a gram.

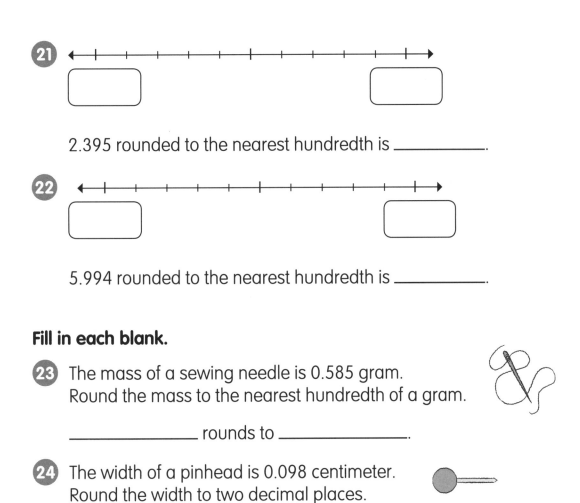

_____ rounds to _____.

24 The width of a pinhead is 0.098 centimeter.
Round the width to two decimal places.

_____ rounds to _____.

25 The width of a pencil eraser is 0.394 inch.
Round the width to the nearest hundredth of an inch.

_____ rounds to _____.

Round each decimal to the nearest whole number, nearest tenth, and nearest hundredth.

26

Decimal	Rounded to the Nearest		
	Whole Number	Tenth	Hundredth
1.049			
2.199			

Fill in each blank.

27 A decimal rounded to the nearest tenth is 2.5.
Write two decimals that can be rounded to 2.5.

_____ and _____

28 A decimal rounded to the nearest hundredth is 4.09.
Write two decimals that can be rounded to 4.09.

_____ and _____

29 A decimal rounded to the nearest hundredth is 6.32.
This decimal is greater than 6.32.

What could this decimal be? _____

30 A decimal rounded to the nearest hundredth is 7.01.
This decimal is less than 7.01.

What could this decimal be? _____

31 What is the least possible decimal that is 9.7 when rounded to

1 decimal place? _____

32 What is the greatest possible decimal that is 5.32 when rounded

to 2 decimal places? _____

Chapter 4 Extra Practice and Homework
Decimals

Activity 3 Decimals, Fractions, and Mixed Numbers

Express each of the following as a decimal.

1 $\frac{3}{8}$ = _____

2 $\frac{19}{8}$ = _____

3 $3\frac{21}{125}$ = _____

4 $15\frac{3}{250}$ = _____

Rewrite each of the following as a fraction or mixed number in simplest form.

5

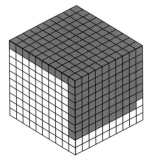

0.169 = _____

6

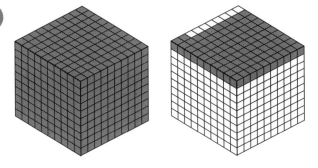

1.092 = _____

7 0.073

8 0.136

9 0.218

10 0.905

11 1.825

12 2.908

13 3.602

14 4.109

Solve.

15 Steven wrote the following:

$6\dfrac{1}{3} = 6.13$

Is he correct? Explain.

_____

_____

1 **Mathematical Habit 7** **Make use of structure**

Explain why 1.8, 1.80, and 1.800 have the same value.

2 **Mathematical Habit 7** **Make use of structure**

Kyle does not know how to find the values of A and B on the number line.
Write the steps Kyle should follow to find the values.

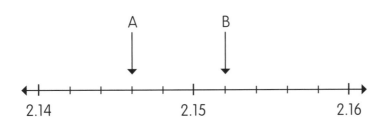

Find the value of each mark on the number line first.

1 **Mathematical Habit 7** **Make use of structure**

You are given two numbers, 3.987 and 70.140.

a Round each number to the nearest tenth.

_____

b Round each number to the nearest hundredth.

_____

c Find the difference between your rounded answers for 3.987.

_____

d Find the difference between your rounded answers for 70.140.

_____

e Are your answers in parts **a** and **b** the same? Explain.

_____

2 **Mathematical Habit 7** **Make use of structure**

a $4.129 = 4 + \dfrac{1}{10} + \dfrac{29}{\boxed{}}$

b $2.075 = 2 + \dfrac{\boxed{}}{1,000} + \dfrac{5}{\boxed{}}$

c $3.157 = \dfrac{\boxed{}}{1,000} + \dfrac{7}{1,000}$

SCHOOL-to-HOME
CONNECTIONS

Four Operations of Decimals

Dear Family,
In this chapter, your child will learn to use the four operations to solve word problems involving decimals. Skills your child will practice include:

- adding, subtracting, and multiplying decimals up to 2 decimal places
- multiplying and dividing decimals up to 3 decimal places by 10, 100, 1,000, their multiples, and powers of 10
- dividing decimals up to 2 decimal places by 1-digit whole numbers
- rounding quotients to the nearest tenth or hundredth
- estimating decimal sums, differences, products, and quotients
- converting from a larger metric unit to a smaller unit, and vice versa
- solving real-world problems

Math Practice
We often encounter decimals in our daily lives, whether we are using money, building, cooking, or competing in sporting events. Knowing how to solve problems that involve decimals is an essential skill. At the end of this chapter, you may want to carry out these activities with your child. These activities will help to strengthen your child's understanding of the four operations of decimals.

Activity 1
- Have your child record the height of each family member in meters.
- Ask your child to find the difference in height between two family members.

Activity 2
- Ask your child to imagine painting his or her room in his or her favorite color.
- Tell your child that Brand A of paint costs $8.35 per can of 500 milliliters and Brand B costs $7.56 per can of 400 milliliters.
- Ask your child which brand of paint is cheaper. (Find the cost per 100 milliliters of each brand. Brand A: $8.35 ÷ 5 = $1.67 per 100 milliliters; Brand B: $7.56 ÷ 4 = $1.89 per 100 milliliters. Brand A is cheaper.)
- Have your child calculate the cost of buying 4.5 liters of the cheaper brand. (4.5 L = 4,500 mL, 4,500 ÷ 500 = 9. Cost of 9 cans of Brand A = $8.35 × 9 = $75.15)
- Ask your child to check his or her answer using estimation. (Round $8.35 to $8. $8 × 9 = $72. So, the answer is reasonable.)

Math Talk

Use the following place-value chart to discuss the value of each digit in each **decimal**.

Ones	.	Tenths	Hundredths
6	.	1	3
3	.	7	2

Talk about the processes of adding and subtracting decimals. Help your child find the sum of the decimals (6.13 + 3.72 = 9.85) and then the difference (6.13 − 3.72 = 2.41).

Ask your child to write any two decimals (up to 2 decimal places), and then **estimate** their sum. Next, have your child find the actual sum to compare. Then, using the same decimals, ask your child to estimate the difference before finding the actual difference. Encourage your child to talk about his or her estimates.

BLANK

Chapter 5
Extra Practice and Homework
Four Operations of Decimals

Activity 1   Adding Decimals

Add. Then, fill in each blank.

1 Add 4.1 and 1.6.

4.1 + 1.6 = _____

```
    4 . 1
+   1 . 6
_____
```

2 Find the sum of 14.25 and 11.73.

14.25 + 11.73 = _____

The sum of 14.25 and 11.73 is _____.

```
    1 4 . 2 5
+   1 1 . 7 3
_____
```

Add.

3
```
    1 0 8 . 3
+   2 4 1 . 2
_____
```

4
```
    7 . 5 4
+   1 . 3 3
_____
```

5
```
    6 4 . 5 0
+   2 3 . 2 5
_____
```

6
```
    4 3 . 8 2
+   5 3 . 1 6
_____
```

Add. Then, fill in each blank.

7 Find the sum of 47.5 and 98.6.

$$47.5 + 98.6 = \underline{\hspace{2cm}}$$

The sum of 47.5 and 98.6 is \underline{\hspace{2cm}}.

```
    4  7 . 5
+   9  8 . 6
_____
```

Add.

8
```
    7 . 6
+   1 . 9
_____
```

9
```
  5  8 . 2
+ 6  2 . 8
_____
```

10
```
  3  6  8 . 0
+ 1  5  7 . 4
_____
```

11
```
  5 . 6  2
+ 4 . 7  9
_____
```

12
```
  8 . 9  3
+ 3 . 4  4
_____
```

13
```
  5  4 . 2  0
+ 3  9 . 8  5
_____
```

14
```
  4  5 . 2  8
+ 7  6 . 0  0
_____
```

15
```
  6  2 . 7  4
+ 5  6 . 3  8
_____
```

Add. Show your work.

16 $6.5 + 8.9 = $ _____

17 $9.07 + 8.96 = $ _____

18 $14.3 + 9.98 = $ _____

19 $47.99 + 8.01 = $ _____

20 **a** $19.6 + 57.34 =$ _____ **b** $36.48 + 72 =$ _____

c $412 + 79.6 =$ _____ **d** $25.9 + 54.81 =$ _____

e $1.68 + 20.9 =$ _____ **f** $57.5 + 44.14 =$ _____

Fill in each blank.

21

```
      6 . 9   3   4
 +   ⬚  ⬚  ⬚  ⬚
 ─────────────────
   1  0 . 6   0   5
```

22 _____ must be added to 0.02 to get 1.

Chapter 5

Extra Practice and Homework
Four Operations of Decimals

Activity 2 Subtracting Decimals

Subtract. Then, fill in each blank.

1 Subtract 3.2 from 8.9.

8.9 − 3.2 = _____

```
    8 . 9
 −  3 . 2
 _____
```

2 Subtract 13.6 from 25.7.

25.7 − 13.6 = _____

```
  2  5 . 7
 −1  3 . 6
 _____
```

3 Find the difference between 6.85 and 7.86.

7.86 − 6.85 = _____

The difference between 6.85 and 7.86

is _____.

```
  7 . 8  6
 −6 . 8  5
 _____
```

Subtract.

4
```
    8  6  5 . 9
 −  5  1  4 . 3
 _____
```

5
```
    6  4  5 . 8
 −  2  1  3 . 0
 _____
```

6
```
    5 4 . 6 8
  - 1 3 . 4 2
  _____
```

7
```
    7 8 . 2 6
  - 4 1 . 0 5
  _____
```

Subtract. Then, fill in each blank.

8 Subtract 1.8 from 3.2.

$3.2 - 1.8 =$ _____

```
    3 . 2
  - 1 . 8
  _____
```

9 Subtract 17.89 from 32.21.

$32.21 - 17.89 =$ _____

```
    3 2 . 2 1
  - 1 7 . 8 9
  _____
```

Subtract.

10
```
    5 . 4
  - 3 . 7
  _____
```

11
```
    3 5 . 6
  - 2 6 . 4
  _____
```

12
```
    4 . 2  3
-   1 . 5  4
_____
```

13
```
    6  5 . 3  8
-   2  9 . 7  3
_____
```

14
```
    4 . 0
-   2 . 7
_____
```

15
```
    2 . 0  0
-   0 . 4  8
_____
```

Subtract. Show your work.

16 67.1 − 13.7 = _____

17 2.3 − 0.48 = _____

18 3 − 0.12 = _____

19 9.5 − 6.05 = _____

20 10 − 2.73 = _____

21 12.1 − 4.68 = _____

22 a   7 − 4.8 = _____

b   50 − 23.6 = _____

c   80 − 45.89 = _____

d   5.11 − 4.5 = _____

e   72.51 − 35.39 = _____

f   84.3 − 36.77 = _____

Chapter 5

Extra Practice and Homework
Four Operations of Decimals

Activity 3   Multiplying Decimals

Multiply.

1 $3 \times 3 =$ _____

$0.3 \times 3 =$ _____

$0.03 \times 3 =$ _____

2 $2 \times 4 =$ _____

$0.2 \times 4 =$ _____

$0.02 \times 4 =$ _____

3 $1 \times 6 =$ _____

$0.1 \times 6 =$ _____

$0.01 \times 6 =$ _____

4 $5 \times 1 =$ _____

$0.5 \times 1 =$ _____

$0.05 \times 1 =$ _____

Multiply. Then, fill in each blank.

5 Multiply 21.2 by 4.

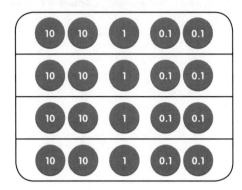

$$\begin{array}{r} 2\ \ 1\ .\ 2 \\ \times\ \ \ \ \ \ \ \ 4 \\ \hline \end{array}$$

21.2 × 4 = _____

6 Find the product of 3.41 and 2.

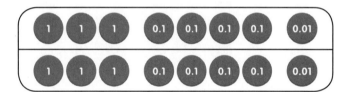

$$\begin{array}{r} 3\ .\ 4\ \ 1 \\ \times\ \ \ \ \ \ \ \ \ 2 \\ \hline \end{array}$$

3.41 × 2 = _____

The product of 3.41 and 2 is _____.

Multiply.

7
$$\begin{array}{r} 2\ .\ 2 \\ \times\ \ \ \ \ 3 \\ \hline \end{array}$$

8
$$\begin{array}{r} 6\ .\ 3 \\ \times\ \ \ \ \ 4 \\ \hline \end{array}$$

Multiply. Show your work.

9 $4.3 \times 2 =$ _____

10 $65.5 \times 2 =$ _____

11 $59.3 \times 4 =$ _____

12 $7.54 \times 7 =$ _____

13 $19.08 \times 6 =$ _____

14 $9 \times 59.84 =$ _____

15 **a** $0.4 \times 3 =$ _____

b $7.9 \times 5 =$ _____

c $12.4 \times 7 =$ _____

d $6.46 \times 9 =$ _____

e $10.07 \times 5 =$ _____

f $15.24 \times 8 =$ _____

Fill in each blank.

16

$$
\begin{array}{r}
\overset{1}{}\,\overset{2}{} \\
6\,.\,\boxed{}\,5 \\
\times \qquad\quad 4 \\
\hline
2\;\;5\,.\,0\;\;0
\end{array}
$$

17 The difference between 12.8×4 and 6.4×8 is _____.

Name: _____ Date: _____

Chapter 5 Extra Practice and Homework
Four Operations of Decimals

Activity 4 Multiplying Decimals by Tens, Hundreds, Thousands, and Powers of Tens

Fill in each blank.

1 a $0.6 \times 10 =$ _____

b $0.37 \times 10 =$ _____

c $8.15 \times 10 =$ _____

d $10 \times 17.52 =$ _____

e $10 \times 0.264 =$ _____

f $10 \times 3.028 =$ _____

2 a $1.907 \times$ _____ $= 19.07$

b $2.74 \times$ _____ $= 27.4$

c _____ $\times 10 = 8.8$

d _____ $\times 10 = 534.2$

3 a $0.3 \times 70 =$ _____

b $0.25 \times 30 =$ _____

c $9.04 \times 60 =$ _____

d $50 \times 13.24 =$ _____

e $90 \times 0.128 =$ _____

f $80 \times 5.179 =$ _____

© 2020 Marshall Cavendish Education Pte Ltd

Extra Practice and Homework Grade 5A

4 Multiplying Decimals by Tens, Hundreds, Thousands, and Powers of Tens

159

4   **a** $0.04 \times 100 =$ _____   **b** $0.18 \times 100 =$ _____

     c $4.9 \times 1,000 =$ _____   **d** $100 \times 16.47 =$ _____

     e $100 \times 0.134 =$ _____   **f** $1,000 \times 63.425 =$ _____

5   **a** $108.1 \times$ _____ $= 10,810$ **b** $50.95 \times$ _____ $= 50,950$

     c   _____ $\times 100 = 909.7$ **d**   _____ $\times 1,000 = 2,350$

6   **a** $0.7 \times 400 =$ _____   **b** $0.36 \times 200 =$ _____

     c $6.09 \times 8,000 =$ _____   **d** $900 \times 10.23 =$ _____

     e $300 \times 0.105 =$ _____   **f** $5,000 \times 3.003 =$ _____

7 $0.75 \times 10^2 = 0.75 \times (10 \times \underline{\hspace{2cm}})$

$= 0.75 \times \underline{\hspace{2cm}}$

$= \underline{\hspace{2cm}}$

8 $0.8 \times 10^2 = 0.8 \times (\underline{\hspace{2cm}} \times 10)$

$= 0.8 \times \underline{\hspace{2cm}}$

$= \underline{\hspace{2cm}}$

9 $0.96 \times 10^2 = 0.96 \times (\underline{\hspace{2cm}} \times 10)$

$= 0.96 \times \underline{\hspace{2cm}}$

$= \underline{\hspace{2cm}}$

10 $0.065 \times 10^2 = 0.065 \times (\underline{\hspace{2cm}} \times 10)$

$= 0.065 \times \underline{\hspace{2cm}}$

$= \underline{\hspace{2cm}}$

11 $13.8 \times 10^2 = 13.8 \times (\underline{\hspace{2cm}} \times \underline{\hspace{2cm}})$

$= 13.8 \times \underline{\hspace{2cm}}$

$= \underline{\hspace{2cm}}$

12 $9.849 \times 10^2 = 9.849 \times (\underline{\hspace{2cm}} \times \underline{\hspace{2cm}})$

$= 9.849 \times \underline{\hspace{2cm}}$

$= \underline{\hspace{2cm}}$

13 $1.3 \times 10^3 = 1.3 \times (10 \times 10 \times \underline{\hspace{2cm}})$

$= 1.3 \times \underline{\hspace{2cm}}$

$= \underline{\hspace{2cm}}$

14 $0.2 \times 10^3 = 0.2 \times ($ _____ $\times 10 \times 10)$

$= 0.2 \times$ _____

$=$ _____

15 $0.06 \times 10^3 = 0.06 \times ($ _____ $\times$ _____ $\times 10)$

$= 0.06 \times$ _____

$=$ _____

16 $12.7 \times 10^3 = 12.7 \times ($ _____ $\times$ _____ $\times 10)$

$= 12.7 \times$ _____

$=$ _____

17 $2.007 \times 10^3 = 2.007 \times ($ _____ $\times$ _____ $\times$ _____ $)$

$= 2.007 \times$ _____

$=$ _____

18 $0.7 \times$ _____ $= 700$

19 $1.5 \times$ _____ $= 150$

20 $3.4 \times$ _____ $= 3,400$

21 $4.12 \times$ _____ $= 412$

22 $5.01 \times$ _____ $= 50.1$

23 _____ $\times 10^2 = 1,220$

24 _____ $\times 10 = 1,818$

25 $3.5 \times 10 = 0.35 \times$ _____

26 $12.9 \times 10^2 =$ _____ $\times 10^3$

Chapter 5 — Extra Practice and Homework
Four Operations of Decimals

Activity 5   Dividing Decimals

Divide.

1 6 ÷ 2 = _____

0.6 ÷ 2 = _____

0.06 ÷ 2 = _____

2 8 ÷ 4 = _____

0.8 ÷ 4 = _____

0.08 ÷ 4 = _____

3 9 ÷ 3 = _____

0.9 ÷ 3 = _____

0.09 ÷ 3 = _____

4 8 ÷ 2 = _____

0.8 ÷ 2 = _____

0.08 ÷ 2 = _____

Divide. Then, fill in each blank.

5 Divide 4.8 by 4.

4.8 ÷ 4 = _____

$$4 \overline{\smash{)}\ 4\ .\ 8}$$

6 Divide 3.96 by 3.

3.96 ÷ 3 = _____

$$3 \overline{)3.96}$$

Divide.

7

$$2 \overline{)28.26}$$

8

$$3 \overline{)63.69}$$

9

$$6 \overline{)606.6}$$

10

$$4 \overline{)484.8}$$

Divide. Show your work.

11 $0.84 \div 3 =$ _____

12 $0.72 \div 6 =$ _____

13 $7.84 \div 4 =$ _____

14 $6.52 \div 2 =$ _____

15 $75.18 \div 6 =$ _____

16 $83.25 \div 9 =$ _____

Divide. Show your work. Round each answer to the nearest tenth.

 a 15 ÷ 4 = _____

b 16 ÷ 3 = _____

c 64 ÷ 6 = _____

d 85 ÷ 9 = _____

Divide. Show your work. Give each answer correct to 2 decimal places.

 18 2 ÷ 3 = _____

19 97 ÷ 3 = _____

20 130 ÷ 9 = _____

21 54.8 ÷ 7 = _____

Divide. Then, fill in each blank.

 Divide 7.96 by 2. Round your answer to the nearest tenth.

$$2 \,\overline{)\,7\,.\,9\,6\,}$$

$7.96 \div 2 =$ _____

 Divide 9.36 by 5. Give your answer correct to 2 decimal places.

$$5 \,\overline{)\,9\,.\,3\,6\,}$$

$9.36 \div 5 =$ _____

Fill in each blank.

 $1.26 \div 3 = 0.42$

So, $0.126 \div 3 =$ _____.

```
          1 . [ ] 3
     ┌──────────────
   5 )  6 . 1 [ ]
        5
      ─────
        1   1
        1   0
      ─────
            1 [ ]
            1 [ ]
          ─────
                0
```

Chapter 5
Extra Practice and Homework
Four Operations of Decimals

Activity 6   Dividing Decimals by Tens, Hundreds, and Thousands

Fill in each blank.

1 $0.2 \div 10 =$ _____

2 $0.84 \div 10 =$ _____

3 $3.19 \div 10 =$ _____

4 $34.95 \div 10 =$ _____

5 $102.8 \div 10 =$ _____

6 $713.02 \div 10 =$ _____

7 $1.84 \div$ _____ $= 0.184$

8 $0.93 \div$ _____ $= 0.093$

9 _____ $\div 10 = 2.705$

10 _____ $\div 10 = 62.09$

11 $4 \div 20 =$ _____

12 $27 \div 60 =$ _____

13 $67.2 \div 70 =$ _____

14 $10.35 \div 50 =$ _____

15 $5.7 \div 100 =$ _____

16 $94.3 \div 100 =$ _____

17 $4,008 \div 100 =$ _____

18 $70 \div 1,000 =$ _____

19 $9,090 \div 1,000 =$ _____

20 $30,400 \div 1,000 =$ _____

21 $90 \div$ _____ $= 0.9$

22 _____ $\div 100 = 0.62$

23 $13,870 \div$ _____ $= 13.87$

24 _____ $\div 1,000 = 2.053$

25 $180 \div 200 =$ _____

26 $201 \div 300 =$ _____

27 $56,640 \div 8,000 =$ _____

28 $15,600 \div 5,000 =$ _____

29 $249,000 \div 6,000 =$ _____

30 $596,400 \div 7,000 =$ _____

31 $48 \div 60 = 0.8$

So, $48 \div 30 =$ _____.

32 $501 \div 30 =$ _____ $\div 100$

Chapter 5 Extra Practice and Homework
Four Operations of Decimals

Activity 7 Estimating Decimals

Add or subtract. Then, estimate to check that each answer is reasonable.

1. $7.6 + 12.3$

2. $21.8 - 11.5$

3. $\$2.90 + \$7.15$

4. $9.05 + 19.55$

5. $35.67 - 15.09$

6. $\$15.40 - \$5.95$

Multiply. Then, estimate to check that each answer is reasonable.

7 4.5 × 4

8 19.6 × 3

9 0.95 × 8

10 8.25 × 3

Divide. Then, estimate to check that each answer is reasonable.

11 24.6 ÷ 5

12 38.4 ÷ 6

13 71.04 ÷ 8

14 99.75 ÷ 5

Calculate. Then, estimate to check that each answer is reasonable.

15 0.47 + 15.51

16 36.54 + 5.87

17 9.95 − 1.46

18 69.23 − 14.84

19 2.89 pounds × 4

20 $1.95 × 8

21 6.34 kilograms ÷ 7

22 11.45 centimeters ÷ 9

Chapter 5

Extra Practice and Homework
Four Operations of Decimals

Activity 8   Converting Metric Units

Fill in each blank.

1 1.53 m = _____ cm

2 2.07 km = _____ m

3 19.875 kg = _____ g

4 3.4 L = _____ mL

5 12.03 m = _____ m _____ cm

6 217.9 km = _____ km _____ m

7 3.64 kg = _____ kg _____ g

8 4.007 L = _____ L _____ mL

9 450 cm = _____ m

10 6,280 m = _____ km

11 7,950 g = _____ kg

12 59 mL = _____ L

13 21 m 7 cm = _____ m

14 42 km 6 m = _____ km

15 9 kg 55 g = _____ kg

16 100 L 850 mL = _____ L

Solve.

17 Maria made the following conversion.

2 L 5 mL = 2.5 L

a Explain what was wrong with her conversion.

_____

_____

b Show the correct conversion.

_____

_____

18 Check (✓) the correct conversions.

a 25 cm = 0.25 m

b 25 m = 0.25 km

c 4 L 20 mL = 4.02 L

d 60 L 200 mL = 60.2 L

e 765 g = 7.65 kg

For those that you did not check, write the correct conversion next to it.

Chapter 5 — Extra Practice and Homework
Four Operations of Decimals

Activity 9   Real-World Problems: Decimals

Solve. Show your work. Use the bar model to help you.

1. Ryan spent $42.65 at a supermarket. He spent $24.50 at a bookshop. How much did Ryan spend altogether?

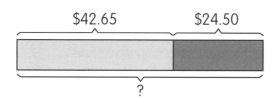

$42.65 $24.50

?

> You can use the four-step problem-solving model to help you.

$_____ ◯ $_____ = $_____

Ryan spent $_____ altogether.

Solve. Show your work. Draw a bar model to help you.

2 Caleb's mass was 34.2 kilograms. He was 15.85 kilograms lighter than his sister. What was his sister's mass?

3 Brady's height was 1.34 meters. He was 0.45 meter taller than his sister. What was Brady's sister's height?

4 Rachel wanted to buy a craft set that cost $58.45, but she was short of $12.90. How much money did Rachel have?

5 The thickness of a piece of wood was 2.45 centimeters. Lucas stacked 9 pieces of wood, one on top of the other. Find the total height of the stack of 9 pieces of wood.

6 One fish tank contained 24.58 liters of water. How much water did 4 of these fish tanks contain?

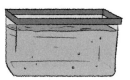

7 Miguel bought 15.4 meters of cloth to sew 7 identical cushion covers. How much cloth did Miguel use for each cushion cover?

8 Ms. Ramirez bought 4 similar blouses. She spent a total of $67. How much did each blouse cost?

Solve. Show your work. Use the bar model to help you.

9 Ali bought 3 similar packets of nuts for $4.65.

   a How much did each packet of nuts cost?

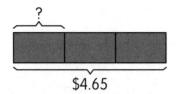

$_____ ◯ _____ = $_____

Each packet of nuts cost $_____.

b How much did 8 of these packets of nuts cost?

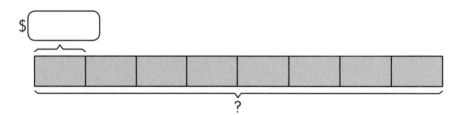

$_____ ◯ _____ = $_____

8 of these packets of nuts cost $_____.

Solve. Show your work. Draw a bar model to help you.

10 David made some fruit punch by mixing mango juice and pineapple juice. He used 2.05 liters of mango juice and twice as much pineapple juice as mango juice to make the fruit punch.

a How much pineapple juice did David use?

b How much fruit punch did David make?

11 Tin A contains 4.08 liters of blue paint. Tin B contains 5.61 liters of white paint. Nathan mixed the paint from both tins. He then used 1.25 liters of the paint. How much paint did Nathan have left?

12 4 similar staplers cost $25. A stapler cost 5 times as much as a box of paper clips. Find the cost of a box of paper clips.

13 Alan used 4.08 meters of cloth to sew a dress. He used 1.2 meters less cloth to sew a skirt. How much cloth did Alan need to sew 5 of these skirts?

14 Brianna saved $9.20 a week for 4 weeks. She needed to save another $15.60 to buy a computer game. What was the price of the computer game?

15 The total mass of 2 similar clay pots and 2 similar metal pots is
13.2 kilograms. The mass of a clay pot is 3 times the mass of a metal pot.
What is the mass of a clay pot?

16 Avery spent a total of $11.60 on 5 similar pens and a ruler.
A ruler cost $1.30 less than a pen. How much did each pen cost?

17 The total distance from Connor's house to his school was 9.18 kilometers. He traveled by bus for part of the journey and walked the rest of the way. The distance he walked was 7.95 kilometers shorter than the distance he traveled by bus. How far did Connor walk?

Name: _____ Date: _____

Mathematical Habit 3 Construct viable arguments

In this chapter, you have learned about decimals and conversion. What is the most difficult part in learning decimals and conversion? Why?

1 **Mathematical Habit** **1** **Persevere in solving problems**

Mr. Gray sold some watches at $14 each and 20 bookmarks at $1.50 each. Ms. Williams sold the same number of watches at $13.50 each and 20 bookmarks at $1.80 each. They collected the same amount of money. How many watches did Mr. Gray sell?

2 **Mathematical Habit** **1** **Persevere in solving problems**

The total volume of 6 bottles of milk and 9 bottles of apple juice was 3.06 liters. The total volume of 3 bottles of milk and 4 bottles of apple juice was 1.44 liters. Find the volume of a bottle of apple juice in liters.